PLANTATIO

EPISODES OF EVERYDAY RACISM

GRADA KILOMBA

BETWEEN THE LINES

TORONTO

Plantation Memories

© Unrast Verlag 2008

First published in North America in 2021 by
Between the Lines
401 Richmond Street West
Studio 281
Toronto, Ontario M5V 3A8
Canada
1-800-718-7201
www.btlbooks.com

Cataloguing in Publication information available from Library and
Archives Canada.
ISBN 9781771135504

Text design by Unrast Verlag
Cover design by DEEVE

Printed in Canada

This is in Remembrance of Our Ancestors

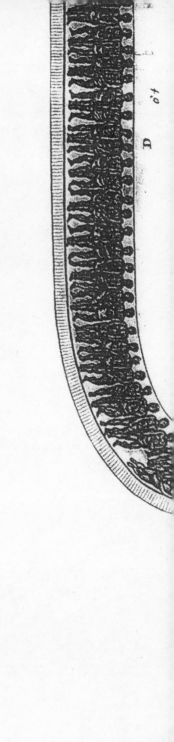

TABLE OF CONTENTS

I do deeply thank

Alicia and *Kathleen* – fictive names – who have shared their very personal stories, memories, joys and injuries with me in the form of interviews, making this book possible.

All my students, who every Wednesday have enthused me with their brilliant questions, observations and thoughts, as well as their incredible dedication and commitment.

Irmingard Staeuble, my first mentor, for her wisdom, kindness and inspiration, as well as for her untiring efforts to motivate me to write and conclude this book.

Paul Mecheril, my second mentor, for his knowledge, humor and clever revelations.

Katharina Oguntoye, for her constant smile, encouragement and politics.

Ursula Wachendorfer, for her moving ideas, tenderness and discussions.

Amy Evans, my dearest friend, who has been inspiring me for a long time, for her beautiful writings, dedication and loving support.

Anne Springer, my psychoanalyst, who has been taking care of my emotional life, wounds, anger and disappointments, giving me the tools to use them as a resource to re-create a happy existence.

Fábio Maia, my Candomblé priest, who has been taking care of my spiritual life, nourishing my soul, my ancestors and my Orixás with care, wisdom and love.

Oxalá or *Obatalá*, my first Orixá, for showing me how to use his serenity, peace, clarity and wisdom as guidance in my life and work.

Yemanjá, my second Orixá, for showing me how to use her love and assertiveness as creative tools.

Oxóssi, my Orixá Odú, for showing me how to catch my dreams with determination and belief, like a hunter.

Oya, my devoted Orixá, for showing me how to use her strength to fight for equality and respect.

And my family: my *father* who, with much love, always told me to become an independent and dignified Black woman. And my *mother* who showed me what it means to be that woman. My grandmother *Vô*. My brothers *Zé*, *Pedro* and *Gonçalo*, and my sisters *Patrícia* and *Júlia*. And, of course, little *André*, little *Keziah* and little *Noah* – the future.

BECOMING THE SUBJECT

> Why do I write?
> 'Cause I have to.
> 'Cause my voice,
> in all its dialects,
> has been silent too long
> (Jacob Sam-La Rose[1])

This is one of my favorite poems. I have read it a thousand times, again and again. And each time I read it, it seems that my whole history is summarized within it. The five short lines recall quite ingeniously a long history of imposed silence. A history of tortured voices, disrupted languages, imposed idioms, interrupted speeches and the many places we could neither enter nor stay to speak our voices. All this seems to be written there. At the same time, this is *not* only a poem about the continual loss urged on by colonialism. It is also a poem about resistance, about a collective hunger to come to voice, to write and to recover our *hidden history*. That is why I like it so much.

The idea that one *has* to write, almost as a virtual moral obligation, embodies the belief that history can "be interrupted, appropriated, and transformed through artistic and literary practice" (hooks 1990: 152). Writing this book has indeed been a way of transforming because here, I am not the 'Other,' but the self, not the object, but the subject, I am the describer of my own history, and not the described. Writing therefore emerges as a political act. The poem illustrates writing as an act of *becoming*,[2] and as I write, I *become* the narrator, and the writer of my own reality, the author of and the authority on my own history. In this sense, I become the absolute opposition of what the colonial project has predetermined.

bell hooks uses these two concepts of 'subject' and 'object,' arguing that subjects are those who alone "have the right to define their own reality, establish their own identities, name their history" (hooks 1989: 42). As objects, however, our reality is defined by others, our identities created by others, and our "history named only in ways that define (our) relationship to those who are subjects" (hooks 1989: 42). This passage from objecthood to subjecthood is what marks writing as a political act. It is furthermore an act of decolonization in that one is opposing colonial positions by becoming the 'valid' and 'legitimate' writer, and reinventing oneself by naming a

---

1 Jacob Sam-La Rose, Poetry, In *Sable: The Literature Magazine for Writers*. Winter 2002, p. 60.

2 The concept of 'becoming' has been used within Cultural and Postcolonial Studies to elaborate the relationship between self and 'Other.'

reality that was either misnamed or not named at all. This book represents this double desire: the desire to oppose that place of 'Otherness' and the desire to invent ourselves anew. Opposition and reinvention thus become two complementary processes, because opposing as such is not enough. One cannot simply oppose racism since in the vacant space after one has opposed and resisted, "there is still the necessity to *become* – to make oneself anew" (hooks 1990: 15). In other words, there is still the need to *become subjects*.

This book can be conceived as a form of 'becoming a subject' because in these writings I seek to bring to voice the psychological reality of everyday racism as told by Black women, based on our subjective accounts, self-perceptions and biographical narratives – in the form of episodes. Here, *we* are speaking "in our own name" (Hall 1990: 222) and about *our* own reality, from *our* own perspective, which has, as in the last line of the poem, been *silent for too long*. This line describes how this process of writing is both a matter of past and of present, that is why I start this book by remembering the past in order to understand the present, and I create a constant dialogue between both, since everyday racism embodies a chronology that is timeless.

Plantation Memories explores the timelessness of everyday racism. The combination of these two words, 'plantation' and 'memories,' describes everyday racism as not only the restaging of a colonial past, but also as a traumatic reality, which has been neglected. It is a violent shock that suddenly places the Black subject in a colonial scene where, as in a plantation scenario, one is imprisoned as the subordinate and exotic 'Other.' Unexpectedly, the past comes to coincide with the present, and the present is experienced as if one were in that agonizing past, as the title of this book announces.

Chapter 1, *The Mask: Colonialism, Memory, Trauma and Decolonization* begins with the description of a colonial instrument, a mask, as a symbol of colonial politics and sadistic *white* policies of silencing the Black subject's voice during slavery: Why must the mouth of the Black subject be fastened? And what would the *white* subject have to listen to? This chapter approaches not only questions related to memory, trauma and speech, but also the construction of Blackness as 'Other.'

Chapter 2, *Who Can Speak? Speaking at the Centre, Decolonizing Knowledge,* approaches similar questions in the context of scholarship: Who can speak? Who can produce knowledge? And whose knowledge is acknowledged as such? In this chapter I explore colonialism in academia and the decolonization of scholarship. In other words, I am concerned here with racial authority and the production of knowledge: what happens when we speak at the centre?

Chapter 3 *Speaking the Unspeakable: Defining Racism.* How should one speak about what has been silenced? Here, I start by analyzing the theoretical deficit in racism and everyday racism theories and explore what for me is the adequate methodology to speak about the experienced reality of everyday racism as told by two women of the African diaspora: Alicia, an Afro-German woman, and Kathleen, an African-American woman living in Germany. Both narrate their experiences of everyday racism within their personal biographies.

Chapter 4, *Gendered Racism: "(...)would you like to clean our house" – Connecting 'Race' and Gender*, is an engendered approach to racism. Here, I explore the intersection between 'race' and gender as well as the failure of Western feminism to approach the reality of Black women within gendered racism. Moreover, I present the aims of Black feminism.

The following chapters constitute the very center of this work. Here, the interviews of Alicia and Kathleen are analyzed in detail in the form of episodes, and divided in the following chapters: chapter 5, *Space Politics*; chapter 6, *Hair Politics*; chapter 7, *Sexual Politics*; chapter 8, *Skin Politics*; chapter 9, *The N-word and Trauma*; chapter 10, *Segregation and Racial Contagion*; chapter 11, *Performing Blackness*; chapter 12, *Suicide*; chapter 13 *Healing and Transformation*.

The book concludes with Chapter 14, *Decolonizing the Self,* where I review and theorize the most important topics that arise in this book as well as possible strategies of decolonization.

CHAPTER 1
THE MASK

COLONIALISM, MEMORY, TRAUMA AND DECOLONIZATION

THE MASK

There is a mask of which I heard many times during my childhood. It was the mask *Escrava Anastácia* was made to wear. The many recounts and the detailed descriptions seemed to warn me that they were not simple facts of the past, but living memories buried in our psyche, ready to be told. Today, I want to re-tell them. I want to speak about that brutal *mask of speechlessness*. This mask was a very concrete piece, a real instrument, which became a part of the European colonial project for more than three hundred years. It was composed of a bit placed inside the mouth of the Black subject, clamped between the tongue and the jaw, and fixed behind the head with two strings, one surrounding the chin and the other surrounding the nose and forehead. Formally, the mask was used by *white* masters to prevent enslaved Africans from eating sugar cane or cocoa beans while working on the plantations, but its primary function was to implement a sense of speechlessness and fear, inasmuch as the mouth was a place of both muteness and torture.

In this sense, the mask represents colonialism as a whole. It symbolizes the sadistic politics of conquest and its cruel regimes of silencing the so-called 'Others': Who can speak? What happens when we speak? And what can we speak about?

THE MOUTH

The mouth is a very special organ, it symbolizes speech and enunciation. Within racism, it becomes the organ of oppression par excellence; it represents the organ *whites* want – and need – to control.

In this particular scenario, the mouth is also a metaphor for possession. It is fantasized that the Black subject wants to possess something that belongs to the *white* master, the fruits: the sugar cane and the cocoa beans. She or he wants to *eat* them, devour them, dispossessing the master of its goods. Although the plantation and its fruits do 'morally' belong to the colonized, the colonizer interprets it perversely, reading it as a sign of robbery. "We are taking what is Theirs" becomes "They are taking what is Ours."

We are dealing here with a process of *denial*, for the master denies its project of colonization and asserts it onto the colonized. It is this moment of

14

SAME RHETORIC USED TODAY!

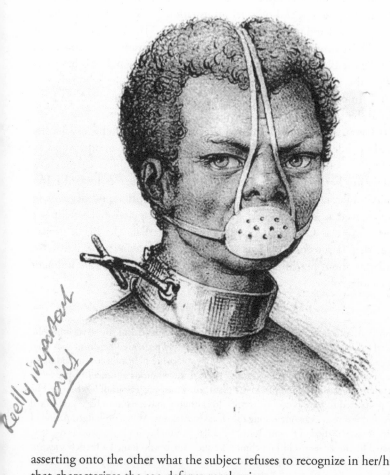

Reelly important point (handwritten)

asserting onto the other what the subject refuses to recognize in her/himself that characterizes the ego defense mechanism.

Escrava Anastácia[3]

---

3 This is a portrait of *Escrava Anastácia* (Slave Anastácia). The penetrant image encounters the viewer with the horrors of slavery endured by generations of enslaved Africans. With no official history, some claim Anastácia was the daughter of a Kimbundo royal family, born in Angola, taken to Bahia (Brazil) and enslaved by a Portuguese family. Upon the family's return to Portugal, she was sold to the owner of a sugar plantation. Others claim she was born a Nagô/Yoruba princess before being captured by European slavers and brought to Brazil, while others point to Bahia as her place of birth. Her African name

→ look for evidence of this! (handwritten)

15

In racism, denial is used to maintain and legitimate violent structures of racial exclusion: "They want to take what is Ours and therefore They have to be controlled." The first and original information – "We are taking what is Theirs" – is denied and projected onto the 'Other' – "They are taking what is Ours" – who becomes what the *white* subject does not want to be acquainted with. While the Black subject turns into the intrusive enemy, who has to be controlled; the *white* subject becomes the sympathetic victim, who is forced to control. In other words, the oppressor becomes the oppressed, and the oppressed, the tyrant.

This is based upon processes in which *split off* parts of the psyche are projected outside, always creating the so-called 'Other' as an antagonist to the 'self.' This splitting evokes the fact that the *white* subject is somehow divided within her/himself, for she/he develops two attitudes toward external reality: only one part of the ego – the 'good,' accepting and benevolent – is experienced as 'self'; the rest – the 'bad,' rejecting and malevolent – is projected onto the 'Other' and experienced as external. The Black subject becomes then a screen of projection for what the *white* subject fears to acknowledge about her/himself: in this case, the violent thief, the indolent and malicious robber.

---

is unknown; Anastácia was the name given to her during enslavement. By all accounts she was forced to wear a heavy iron collar and a facemask that prevented her from speaking. The reasons given for this punishment vary: some report her political activism aiding in the escape of other slaves; others claim she resisted the amorous advances of her *white* master; and yet another version places the blame on a mistress jealous of her beauty. She is often purported to have possessed tremendous healing powers and to have performed miracles, and was seen as a saint among the enslaved Africans. After a prolonged period of suffering, Anastácia died of tetanus from the collar around her neck. Anastácia's drawing was created by the 27-year-old Frenchman Jacques Arago who joined a French *scientific expedition* to Brazil as its draftsman between December 1817 and January 1818. There are other drawings of masks covering the entire face with two holes for the eyes; these were used to prevent *dirt eating*, a practice among enslaved Africans to commit suicide. In the latter half of the 20th century the figure of Anastácia began to be the symbol of slavery brutality and its continuing legacy of racism. Anastácia became an important political and religious figure all over the African and African Diasporic world, representing heroic resistance. The first wide-scale veneration began in 1967 when the curators of Rio's *Museu do Negro* (Black Museum) erected an exhibition to honor the 80th anniversary of the abolition of slavery in Brazil. She is commonly seen as a saint of the *Pretos Velhos* (Old Black Slaves), directly related to the Orixá Oxalá or Obatalá – the God of peace, serenity, creation and wisdom – and is an object of devotion in the Candomblé and Umbanda religions (Handler & Hayes 2009).

Such dishonorable aspects, whose intensity causes too much anxiety, guilt or shame, are projected outside as a means of escaping them. In psychoanalytical terms, this allows positive feelings toward oneself to remain intact – whiteness as the 'good' self – while the manifestations of the 'bad' self are projected onto the outside and seen as external 'bad' objects. In the *white* conceptual world, the Black subject is identified as the *'bad' object*, embodying those aspects that *white* society has repressed and made taboo, that is, aggression and sexuality. We therefore come to coincide with the threatening, the dangerous, the violent, the thrilling, the exciting and also the dirty, but desirable, allowing whiteness to look at itself as morally ideal, decent, civilized and majestically generous, in complete control, and free of the anxiety its historicity causes.

THE WOUND[4]

Within this unfortunate dynamic, the Black subject becomes not only the 'Other' – the difference against which the *white* 'self' is measured – but also 'Otherness' – the personification of the repressed aspects of the *white* 'self.' In other words, we become the mental representation of what the *white* subject does not want to be like. Toni Morrison (1992) uses the expression 'unlikeness' to describe whiteness as a dependent identity that exists through the exploitation of the 'Other,' a relational identity constructed by *whites* defining themselves as unlike racial 'Others.' That is, Blackness serves as the primary form of Otherness by which whiteness is constructed. The 'Other' is not other *per se*; it becomes such through a process of absolute denial. In this sense, Frantz Fanon writes:

What is often called the Black soul is a *white* man's artifact (1967: 110)

This sentence reminds us that it is not the Black subject we are dealing with, but *white* fantasies of what Blackness should be like. Fantasies, which do not represent us, but the *white* imaginary. They are the denied aspects of the *white* self which are re-projected onto us, as if they were authoritative and objective pictures of ourselves. They are however not of our concern. 'I cannot go to a film' writes Fanon, 'I wait for me' (1967: 140). He waits

---

4 The term 'trauma' is derived from the Greek word 'wound' (Laplanche & Pontalis 1988), and it is in this sense that I use it here: wound as trauma.

for the Black savages, the Black barbarians, the Black servants, the Black prostitutes, whores and courtesans, the Black criminals, murderers and drug dealers. He waits for what he is not.

We could actually say that in the *white* conceptual world, it is as if the collective unconscious of Black people is pre-programmed for alienation, disappointment and psychic trauma, since the images of Blackness we are confronted with are neither realistic nor gratifying. What an alienation, to be forced to identify with heroes who are *white* and reject enemies who appear as Black. What a disappointment, to be forced to look at ourselves *as if we were in their place*. What a pain, to be trapped in this colonial order.

This should be our preoccupation. We should not worry about the *white* subject in colonialism, but rather about the fact that the Black subject is always forced to develop a relationship to her/himself through the alienating presence of the *white* other (Hall 1996). Always placed as the 'Other,' never as the self.

'What else could it be for me,' asks Fanon, 'but an amputation, an excision, a hemorrhage that spattered my whole body with black blood?' (1967: 112). He uses the language of trauma, like most Black people when speaking of their everyday experiences of racism, indicating the painful bodily impact and loss characteristic of a traumatic collapse, for within racism one is surgically removed, violently separated, from whatever identity one might really have. Such separation is defined as classic trauma, since it deprives one of one's own link with a society unconsciously thought of as *white*. 'I felt knife blades open within me ... I could no longer laugh' (1967:112), he remarks. There is indeed nothing to laugh about, as one is being overdetermined from the outside by violent fantasies one sees, but one does not recognize as being oneself.

This is the trauma of the Black subject; it lies exactly in this state of absolute Otherness in relation to the *white* subject. An infernal circle: 'When people like me, they tell me it is in spite of my color. When they dislike me, they point out that it is not because of my color,' Fanon writes. 'Either way, I am locked' (1967: 116). Locked within unreason. It seems then that Black people's trauma stems not only from family-based events, as classical psychoanalysis argues, but rather from the traumatizing contact with the violent unreason of the *white* world, that is, with the unreason of racism that places us always as 'Other,' as different, as incompatible, as conflicting, as strange and uncommon. This unreasonable reality of racism is described by Frantz Fanon as traumatic.

I was hated, despised, detested, not by the neighbor across the street or my cousin on my mother's side, but by an entire race. I was up against something unreasoned. The psychoanalysts say that nothing is more traumatizing for the young child than this encounters with what is rational. I would personally say that for a man whose weapon is reason there is nothing more neurotic than contact with unreason (Fanon 1967: 118).

Later he continues, 'I had rationalized the world and the world had rejected me on the basis of color prejudice (...) it was up to the white man to be more irrational than I' (1967: 123). It would seem that the unreason of racism is trauma.

SPEAKING THE SILENCE

The mask, therefore, raises many questions: Why must the mouth of the Black subject be fastened? Why must she or he be silenced? What could the Black subject say if her or his mouth were not sealed? And what would the *white* subject have to listen to? There is an apprehensive fear that if the colonial subject speaks, the colonizer will have to listen. She/he would be forced into an uncomfortable confrontation with 'Other' truths. Truths that have been denied, repressed and kept quiet, as secrets. I do like this phrase "quiet as it's kept." It is an expression of the African Diasporic people that announces how someone is about to reveal what is presumed to be a secret. Secrets like slavery. Secrets like colonialism. Secrets like racism.

The *white* fear of listening to what could possibly be revealed by the Black subject can be articulated by Sigmund Freud's notion of *repression*, since the 'essence of repression,' he writes, 'lies simply in turning something away, and keeping it at distance, from the conscious' (1923: 17). It is that process by which unpleasant ideas – and unpleasant truths – are rendered unconscious, out of awareness, due to the extreme anxiety, guilt or shame they cause. However, while buried in the unconscious as secrets, they remain latent and capable of being revealed at any moment. The mask sealing the mouth of the Black subject prevents the *white* master from listening to those latent truths she/he wants 'to turn away,' 'keep at a distance,' at the margins, uunoticed and 'quiet.' So to speak, it protects the *white* subject from acknowledging 'Other' knowledge. Once confronted with the collective secrets and the unpleasant truths of that very *dirty history*,[5] the *white* subject commonly argues: 'not to know...,' 'not to understand...,' 'not to remember...,' 'not to believe...' or 'not to be convinced by....' These are expressions of this process of repression by which the subject resists making the unconscious information conscious; that is, one wants to make the known unknown.

Repression is, in this sense, the defense by which the ego controls and exercises censorship of what is instigated as an 'unpleasant' truth. Speaking becomes then virtually impossible, as when we speak, our speech is often interpreted as a dubious interpretation of reality, not imperative enough to be either spoken or listened to. This impossibility illustrates how speaking and silencing emerge as an analogous project. The act of speaking is like a negotiation between those who speak and those who listen, between the speaking subjects and their listeners (Castro Varela & Dhawan 2003). Listening is, in this sense, the act of authorization toward the speaker. One can (only) speak when one's voice is listened to. Within this dialect, those who are listened to are those who 'belong.' And those who are *not* listened to become those who 'do *not* belong.' The mask re-creates this project of silencing, controlling the possibility that the Black subject might one day be listened to and consequently might belong.

In a public speech Paul Gilroy[6] described five different ego defense mechanisms the *white* subject goes through in order to be able to 'listen,' that is in order to become aware of its own whiteness and of itself as a performer of racism: denial / guilt / shame / recognition / reparation. Even though Gilroy did not explain this chain of ego defense mechanisms, I would like to do so here, as it is both important and enlightening.

Denial, is an ego defense mechanism that operates unconsciously to resolve emotional conflict, by refusing to admit the more unpleasant aspects of external reality and internal thoughts or feelings. It is the refusal to acknowledge the truth. Denial is followed by two other ego defense mechanisms: splitting and projection. As I wrote earlier, the subject denies that she/he has such-and-such feelings, thoughts or experiences, but goes on to assert that someone else does. The original information – "We are taking what is Theirs" or "We are racist" – is denied and projected onto the 'Others': "They come here and take what is Ours," "They are racist." To diminish emotional shock and grief, the Black subject would say: "We are indeed taking what is

---

5 A sentence commonly used by Toni Morrison to describe her artistic work. As she argues, her writings bring into light the so-called 'dirty business of racism' (1992).

6 *Der Black Atlantic*, in the Haus der Kulturen der Welt, Berlin, 2004.

Theirs" or "I never experienced racism." Denial is often confused with *negation*; these are, however, two different ego defense mechanisms. In the latter, a feeling, thought or experience is admitted to the conscious in its negative form (Laplanche & Pontalis 1988). For instance: "We are not taking what is Theirs" or "We are not racist."

After denial is *guilt*, the emotion that follows the infringement of a moral injunction. It is an affective state in which one experiences conflict at having done something that one believes one should not have done, or the way around, having not done something one believes one should have done. Freud describes this as the result of a conflict between the ego and the super-ego, that is, a conflict between one's own aggressive wishes toward others and the super-ego (authority). The subject is not trying to assert on others what she/he fears to acknowledge in her/himself, like in denial, but is instead pre-occupied with the consequences of her/his own infringement: 'accusation,' 'blame,' 'punishment.' Guilt differs from *anxiety* in that anxiety is experienced in relation to a future occurrence, such as the anxiety created by the idea that racism might occur. Guilt is experienced in relation to an act already committed, that is, racism has already occured, creating an affective state of guiltiness. The common responses to guilt are *intellectualization* or *rationalization*, that is the *white* subject tries to construct a logical justification for racism; or *disbelief* as the *white* subject might say: "we didn't mean it that way," "you misunderstood," "for me, there is no Black or *white*, we are all just people." Suddenly, the *white* subject invests both intellectually and emotionally in the idea that "'race' does not really matter," as a strategy to reduce the unconscious aggressive wishes toward 'Others' and the sense of guilt.

Shame, on the other hand, is the fear of ridicule, the response to the failure to live up to one's ego ideal. While guilt occurs if one transgresses an injunction derived from outside oneself, shame occurs if one fails to achieve an ideal of behavior one has set for oneself. Shame is therefore closely connected to the sense of insight. It is provoked by experiences that call into question our pre-conceptions about ourselves and compel us to see ourselves through the eyes of others, helping us to recognize the discrepancy between other people's perceptions of us and our own conception of ourselves: "Who am I? How do others perceive me? And what do I represent to them?" The *white* subject realizes that the perception Black people have of whiteness might be different than its own self-perception, as whiteness is seen as a privileged identity, which signifies both power and alarm – shame is the result of this conflict.

Recognition follows shame; it is the moment when the *white* subject recognizes its own whiteness and/or racisms. It is, therefore, a process of acknowledgment. One finally acknowledges reality by accepting the reality and perception of others. Recognition is, in this sense, the passage from fantasy to reality – it is no longer a question of how I would like to be seen, but rather of who I am; not what I would like 'Others' to be, but rather who they really are.

Reparation then means the negotiation of recognition. One negotiates reality. In this sense, it is the act of repairing the harm caused by racism by changing structures, agendas, spaces, positions, dynamics, subjective relations, vocabulary, that is, giving up privileges.

These different steps reveal racism awareness not so much as a moral issue but rather as a psychological process that demands work. In this sense, instead of asking the common moral question: "Am I racist?" and expecting a comfortable answer, the *white* subject should rather ask: "How can I dismantle my own racisms?", as the question itself initiates that process.

CHAPTER 2

WHO CAN SPEAK?

SPEAKING AT THE CENTRE, DECOLONIZING KNOWLEDGE

"CAN THE SUBALTERN SPEAK?"

Gayatri C. Spivak (1995) poses the question, 'Can the subaltern speak?' To which she replies, 'No!' It is impossible for the subaltern to speak or to recover her/his voice, for even if she or he tried with all her/his strength and violence, her/his voice would still not be listened to or understood by those in power. In this sense, the subaltern cannot really speak; she/he is always confined to the position of marginality and silence that postcolonialism prescribes.

Spivak uses widow immolation in India as a symbol of the subaltern. The Indian widow, she argues, is incarcerated within both colonialism and patriarchy, making it almost impossible for her to come to voice. The act of burning the widow on her husband's pyre, she continues, confirms that they are absent as subjects. This absence symbolizes the position of the subaltern as an oppressed subject who cannot speak because the structures of oppression neither permit these voices to be heard, nor provide a space for their articulation. At this point, Spivak offers a very meaningful insight as she is questioning the notion of *speaking*. When she argues that the subaltern cannot speak, she is not referring to the act of speaking itself; it does not mean that we cannot articulate speech or that we cannot speak in our own name. Spivak instead refers to the difficulty of speaking within the repressive regime of colonialism and racism. Some years later, we posed a similar question in the German context: "*Spricht die Subalterne deutsch?*" (Steyerl & Gutiérrez Rodríguez 2003).

Spivak's position on the *silent subaltern* is, however, problematic if seen as an absolute statement about colonial relations, because it sustains the idea that the Black subject has no ability to question and counter colonial discourses. This position, argues Benita Parry (quoted in Loomba 1998), deliberates deafness to the native voice *where it can be heard* and attributes an absolute power to the *white* dominant discourse. The idea of a subaltern who cannot speak, as Patricia Hill Collins (2000) explains, first encounters the colonial ideology that subordinate groups identify unconditionally with the powerful and have no valid independent interpretation of their own oppression – and thus cannot speak. Secondly, the idea of a *silent subaltern* can also entail the colonial claim that subordinate groups are less human than their rulers and are therefore less capable of speaking in their own name. Both claims see the colonized as incapable of speaking and our speeches as unsatisfactory and inadequate, and, in this sense, soundless. They also encounter the common suggestion that oppressed groups lack motivation for political activism because of a flawed consciousness of their own subordination. Yet, the subaltern – the colonized – has been neither a passive victim nor a willing accomplice to domination.

It is unnecessary to choose between the positions of whether one can speak or not. Spivak, however, warns postcolonial critics against romanticizing the resistant subjects. She takes seriously the desire of postcolonial intellectuals to emphasize oppression and provide the perspective of the oppressed. But her point is to challenge the easy assumption that we can recover the standpoint of the subaltern. The very absence of the voice of the colonized (from the centre) can be read as emblematic of the difficulty of recovering the voice of the colonial subject and confirmation that there is *no space* where the colonized can speak.

KNOWLEDGE AND THE MYTH OF THE UNIVERSAL

Every semester, on the very first day of my seminar, I quiz my students to give them a sense of how knowledge and racial power intertwine. We first count how many people are in the room. Then I start by asking very simple questions: What was the Berlin Conference of 1884-5? Which African countries were colonized by Germany? How many years did German colonization in the continent of Africa last? I conclude with more specific questions: Who was Queen Nzinga and what role did she play in the struggle against European colonization? Who wrote *Black Skin, White Masks*? Who was May Ayim?

Not surprisingly, most of the *white* students seated in the room are unable to answer the questions, while the Black students answer most of them successfully. Suddenly, those who are usually unseen become visible, while those who are always seen become invisible. Those who are usually silent start speaking, while those who always speak become silent. Silent, not because they cannot articulate their voices or their tongues, but rather because they do not possess *that* knowledge. Who knows what? Who doesn't? And why?

This exercise allows us to visualize and understand how concepts of knowledge, scholarship and science are intrinsically linked to power and racial authority. What knowledge is being acknowledged as such? And what knowledge is not? What knowledge has been made part of academic agendas? And what knowledge has not? Whose knowledge is this? Who is acknowledged to have the knowledge? And who is not? Who can teach knowledge? And who cannot? Who is at the centre? And who remains outside, at the margins?

These questions are important to ask because the centre, which I refer to here as the academic centre, is not a neutral location. It is a *white* space where

Black people have been denied the privilege to speak. Historically, it is a space where we have been voiceless and where *white* scholars have developed theoretical discourses that formally constructed us as the inferior 'Other,' placing Africans in absolute subordination to the *white* subject. Here we have been described, classified, dehumanized, primitivized, brutalized, killed. This is not a neutral space. Within these rooms we were made the objects "of predominantly *white* aesthetic and cultural discourses" (Hall 1992: 252), but we have rarely been the subjects. This position of objecthood that we commonly occupy, this place of 'Otherness,' does not, as commonly believed, indicate a lack of resistance or interest, but rather a lack of access to representation on the part of Blacks themselves. It is not that we have not been speaking, but rather our voices – through a system of racism – have been either systematically disqualified as invalid knowledge; or else represented by *whites* who, ironically, become the 'experts' on ourselves. Either way, we are caught in a violent colonial order. In this sense, academia is neither a neutral space nor simply a space of knowledge and wisdom, of science and scholarship, but also a space of v – i – o – l – e – n – c – e.

As a scholar, for instance, I am commonly told that my work on everyday racism is very interesting, but not really scientific, a remark that illustrates the colonial order in which Black scholars reside: "You have a very *subjective* perspective"; "very *personal*"; "very *emotional*"; "very *specific*"; "Are these *objective facts*?" Such comments function like a mask, that silences our voices as soon as we speak. They allow the *white* subject to place our discourses back at the margins, as deviating knowledge, while their discourses remain at the centre, as the norm. When they speak it is scientific, when we speak it is unscientific;

universal / specific;
objective / subjective;
neutral / personal;
rational / emotional;
impartial / partial;
they have facts, we have opinions;
they have knowledge, we have experiences.

These are not simple semantic categorizations; they possess a dimension of power that maintains hierarchical positions and upholds *white* supremacy. We are not dealing here with a "peaceful coexistence of words," as Jacques Derrida (1981: 41) emphasizes, but rather a violent hierarchy that defines *who can speak*.

KNOWLEDGE AND THE MYTH OF OBJECTIVITY

For a long time we have been speaking and producing independent knowledge, but when groups are unequal in power, they are likewise unequal in their access to the resources necessary to implement their own voices (Collins 2000). Because we lack control over such structures, the articulation of our own perspective outside the group becomes extremely difficult, if not unrealizable. As a result, the work of Black writers and scholars often remains outside the academic body and its agendas, as the quiz has shown. These are not accidentally there; they are placed at the margins by dominant regimes that regulate what 'true' scholarship is. And considering that knowledge is colonized, argues Irmingard Staeuble, and that colonialism "not only meant the imposition of Western authority over indigenous lands, indigenous modes of production and indigenous law and government, but the imposition of Western authority over all aspects of indigenous knowledges, languages and cultures," it is not only an immense but urgent task to decolonize the eurocentric order of knowledge (2007: 90).

Moreover, the structures of knowledge validation, which define what 'true' and 'valid' scholarship is, are controlled by *white* scholars, both male and female, who declare their perspectives universal requirements. As long as Black people and People of Color are denied positions of authority and command in the academy, the idea of what science and scholarship are prevails intact, remaining the exclusive and unquestionable 'property' of whiteness. Thus, it is not an objective scientific truth that we encounter in the academy, but rather the result of unequal power 'race' relations.

Any scholarship that does not convey the eurocentric order of knowledge has been continuously rejected on the grounds that it does not constitute credible science. Science is, in this sense, not a simple apolitical study of truth, but the reproduction of racial power relations that define what counts as true and in whom to believe. The themes, paradigms and methodologies of traditional scholarship – the so-called epistemology – reflect not a diverse space for theorization, but rather the specific political interests of *white* society (Collins 2000, Nkweto Simmonds 1997). Epistemology, as derived from the Greek words *episteme,* meaning knowledge and *logos,* meaning science, is the science of the acquisition of knowledge. It determines which questions merit to be questioned (themes), how to analyze and explain a phenomenon (paradigms), and how to conduct research to produce knowledge (methods), and in this sense defines not only what true scholarship is, but also whom to believe and whom to trust. But who defines which questions merit being asked? Who is asking them? Who is explaining them? And to whom are the answers directed?

Due to racism, Black people experience a reality different from *white* people and we therefore question, interpret and evaluate this reality differently. The themes, paradigms and methodologies used to explain such reality might differ from the themes, paradigms and methodologies of the dominant. It is this 'difference,' however, that is distorted from what counts as valid knowledge. Here, I inevitably have to ask how I, as a Black woman, can produce knowledge in an arena that systematically constructs the discourses of Black scholars as less valid.

KNOWLEDGE AND THE MYTH OF NEUTRALITY

Interesting, but *unscientific*; interesting, but *subjective*; interesting, but *personal, emotional* and *partial*: "You do *over-interpret*," said a colleague. "You must think you are the *queen of interpretation*." Such comments reveal the endless control over the Black subject's voice and the longing to govern and command how we approach and interpret reality. With these remarks, the *white* subject is assured of her/his sense of power and authority over a group that she/he is labeling 'less knowledgeable.'

The last comment, in particular, has two powerful moments. The first is a form of warning which describes the standpoint of the Black woman as a distortion of the truth, expressed here through the word 'over-interpretation.' The *white* female colleague was warning me that I am reading over, beyond the norms of traditional epistemology, and am therefore producing invalid knowledge. It seems to me that this idea of over-interpretation addresses the thought that the oppressed is seeing 'something' that is not to be seen and is about to say 'something' that is not to be said, 'something' that should be kept quiet, secret.

Curiously, in feminist discourse, men similarly try to irrationalize the thinking of women, as if such feminist interpretations were nothing but a fabrication of reality, an illusion, maybe even a female hallucination. Within the former constellation, it is the *white* woman who is irrationalizing my own thinking and in doing so defining *to* a Black woman what 'real' scholarship is and how it should be expressed. This reveals the complex dynamic between 'race,' gender and power, and how the assumption of a world divided into powerful men and subordinate women cannot explain *white* women's power over both Black women and men.

In the second moment, she speaks then of hierarchical positions, of a queen she fantasizes I want to be, but cannot become. The queen is an interesting metaphor. It is a metaphor for power. A metaphor also for the idea that certain bodies belong to certain places: a queen naturally belongs to the palace 'of knowledge,' unlike the plebeians, who can never achieve a position of royalty. They are sealed in their subordinate bodies. Such a hierarchy introduces a dynamic in which Blackness signifies not only 'inferiority' but also '*being out of place*' while whiteness signifies '*being in place*' and therefore 'superiority.' I am told to be out of my place, for in her fantasy I cannot be the queen, but only the plebeian. She seems to be concerned with my body as improper. Within racism, Black bodies are constructed as improper bodies, as bodies that are '*out of place*' and therefore as bodies which cannot belong. *White* bodies, on the contrary, are constructed as proper; they are bodies '*in place*,' '*at home*,' bodies that always belong. They belong everywhere: in Europe, in Africa; North, South; East, West, at the centre as well as at the periphery. Through such comments, Black scholars are persistently invited to return to 'their place,' 'outside' academia, at the margins, where their bodies are seen as 'proper' and 'at home.' Such aggressive comments are a fruitful performance of power, control and intimidation that certainly succeed in silencing oppressed voices. Fruitful indeed, for I remember I stopped writing for more than a month. I became temporarily voiceless. I had had a *white-out*, and was waiting for a *Black-in*.

So I kept remembering Audre Lorde's words:

> And when we speak
> we are afraid our words will not be heard
> nor welcomed
> but when we are silent
> we are still afraid.
> So it is better to speak
> remembering
> we were never meant to survive.

MARGINAL DISCOURSES – PAIN, DISAPPOINTMENT AND ANGER

Of course speaking about these positions of marginality evokes pain, disappointment and anger. They are reminders of the places we can hardly enter, the places at which we either never 'arrive' or 'can't stay' (hooks 1990: 148).

Such reality must be spoken and theorized. It must have a place within discourse because we are not dealing here with 'private information.' Such apparently 'private information' is not private at all. These are not personal stories or intimate complaints, but rather accounts of racism. Such experiences reveal the inadequacy of dominant scholarship in relating not only to marginalized subjects, but also to our experiences, discourses and theorizations. They mirror the historical, political, social and emotional realities of 'race relations' within academic spaces and should therefore be articulated in both theory and methodology.

I therefore call for an epistemology that includes the personal and the subjective as part of academic discourse, for we all speak from a specific time and place, from a specific history and reality – there are no neutral discourses. When *white* scholars claim to have a neutral and objective discourse, they are not acknowledging the fact that they too write from a specific place, which, of course, is neither neutral nor objective or universal, but dominant.[7] It is a place of power. So, if these essays seem preoccupied with narrating emotions and subjectivity as part of theoretical discourse, it is worth remembering that theory is always placed somewhere and always written by someone. My writings might be embedded in emotion and subjectivity as, contrary to traditional scholarship, Black scholars name themselves as well as the place from where they are writing, creating a new discourse with a new language. I, as a Black woman, write with words that describe my reality, not with words that describe the reality of a *white* scholar, for we write from different places. I write from the periphery, not from the centre. This is also the place from where I am theorizing, as I place my discourse within my own reality. The speech of Black scholars then often arises as a lyrical and theoretical discourse that transgresses the language of classic scholarship. A discourse that is as political as it is personal and poetic, like Frantz Fanon's writings or bell hooks. This should be the primary concern of scholarship's decolonization "to bring out a chance for alternative emancipatory knowledge production," as Irmingard Staeuble argues, to transform "the configurations of knowledge and power for the sake of opening up new spaces for theorizing and practice" (2007: 90). As Black writers and scholars, we are transforming configurations of both knowledge and power as we are moving between oppressive boundaries, between the margin and the centre. This transformation is mirrored in our

---

7 The involvement of science in racist constructions is such that it has "made clear that (its) universalistic claims lack any basis as to objectivity or value neutrality" (Staeuble 2007: 89).

discourses. When we produce knowledge, argues bell hooks, our discourses embody not only words of struggle, but also of pain – the pain of oppression. And when hearing our discourses, one can also hear the pain and emotion contained within its brokenness: the brokenness, she argues, of *still* being excluded from places at which we have just 'arrived,' but can hardly 'stay.'

I recall my registration process at the university for my doctorate project as a moment of pain. It aroused the pain of both coming from the margins and the 'im-possibility' of entering the centre. Registration, so emblematic of my passage to the centre, was a long and dubious process that appeared impossible to overcome or to triumph. I remember how the list of documents required to register changed every time the process seemed to be completed. I was asked over and over again for new certificates that had neither been listed nor even mentioned before. Collecting these consumed immense time and money, going back and forth, sending faxes, requesting papers, waiting for authenticated documents from my country, translating them into German, and authenticating the translations again. In the end, I was told that none of these documents were actually necessary, but rather a German language exam. It was the first time anyone had mentioned that in order to be immatriculated as a Ph.D. scholar, I would have to take a German language exam. The exam would take place two days later. I was astonished that I had never been told; at least then I could have prepared. The exam, however, was not listed as an official requirement for a Ph.D. and I told them, to no avail. Two days later, I sat unprepared in an enormous room with dozens of students from all over the world. The tension was grotesque. The exam would determine who could become a student and remain in Germany and who could not. After the exam, I searched for the university bylaws, asked for a translation and carefully read all the sections of the constitution. Indeed I did not need this exam. There was no neutrality! There was no objectivity! This space was not an 'impartial' one!

It seemed I had at last met all the necessary conditions to register. When I finally had my last appointment with one of the head directors at the registration office, she sat in front of me, my documents in her hands, and persuasively asked *if I was really sure* that *I wanted* to *register* as a Ph.D. scholar. She explained that *I did not have to*, and added that I should consider the possibility of researching and writing my dissertation at home. The 'home' she was referring to is asserted here as the margins. I was being asked to remain 'at home,' 'outside' the university structures, with the unofficial status of researcher. The *white* woman, on the other hand, was speaking from the inside – from the centre – where she was both documented and official. Racial difference comes to coincide with spatial difference, as the *white* woman, who inhabits the centre, asks the Black woman, who is at the periphery, not to enter but instead to remain at the margins. The unequal power relations of 'race' are then rearticulated in the unequal power relations between spaces (Mohanram 1999: 3). I was furious and exhausted. How many obstacles still? How many lies and misunderstandings? Who can indeed enter this centre? And who has the *permission* to produce knowledge?

Because my registration process took so long and I still didn't possess the usual matriculation card, my head mentor kindly and promptly wrote an official letter saying I was her Ph.D. student. This would provide me access to the university structure. I used to carry this letter with me, inside my wallet. The very first time I visited the Psychology library at the Free University in Berlin, right at the entrance as I was walking in, I was suddenly called over by a *white* female employee, who said aloud: "You are not from here, are you? The library is only for university students!" Perplexed, I stopped. Among the several dozen *white* people circulating 'inside' that enormous room, I was the only one who was stopped and checked at the entrance. How could she know whether I was 'from there' or 'from elsewhere'? By saying "only for university students," the library employee was informing me that my body was not *read* as an academic body. The university students she was referring to were the *white* others in the room. In her eyes, they were read as academic bodies, bodies 'in place,' 'at home,' as previously mentioned. I responded by showing her the letter, which, like a passport, would also make me 'a body in place.' The paper would allow me to enter a space that my skin did not. Here, Blackness comes to coincide not only with 'outside,' but also with immobility. I am immobilized, because as a Black woman I am seen as being 'out of place.' The ability that *white* bodies have to move freely in the room results from the fact that they are always 'in place' – in the unmarking of *white*ness (Ahmed 2000). Blackness, on the other hand, is signified through marking. I am marked as both different and incompetent: different – "You're not from here" – incompetent – "only for university students" – and thus immobilized – "Are you really sure you want to register as a Ph.D. student?"

DECOLONIZING KNOWLEDGE

Writing about one's own body and exploring the signifiers of the body can, of course, be seen as an act of narcissism or of essentialism, writes Felly Nkweto Simmonds (1997). She concludes, however, that it is an important strategy African and African Diasporic women use to deconstruct their position within academia. The episodes above explore not only the problematic relationship between academia and Blackness, but also the relationship between us and the social theory that provides for our embodied experiences. As Gayatri C. Spivak explains in her essay *Marginality in the Teaching Machine*, such personal writings are a "persistent (de)constructive critique of theory" (Spivak 1993: 3), a debate about the impossibility of escaping the body and its racist constructions inside the 'teaching machine.' Because one is not simply 'a fish in the water'; this water has weight:

> I cannot be, as Bourdieu[8] suggests, a fish in water that 'does not feel the weight of the water, and takes the world about itself for granted. The world that I inhabit as an academic is a *white* world. (...) Academic discourses of the social have constructed blackness as the inferior 'other,' so that even when blackness is named, it contains a problem of relationality to *white*ness. (...) In this *white* world I am a fresh water fish that swims in sea water. I feel the weight of the water... on my body (Nkweto Simmonds 1997: 226-7).

I too feel the weight of this water. During the registration process, I often considered leaving Germany or giving up my dissertation project, like a few other Black colleagues of mine did at that time.[9] This paradoxical situation describes the dynamic between 'race' and space described above. Would I have to leave the country to do scholarly work? Or could I stay inside the country, but outside scholarship? Would I manage to both remain inside the country and inside scholarship? And how much would that cost me emotionally, to be one of the few Black scholars inside this *white* machinery? Those questions were revolving constantly in my mind.

---

8 Nkweto Simmonds previously quotes Bourdieu: "Social reality exists, so to speak, twice, in the things and in minds, in fields and in habitus, outside and inside of agents. And when habitus encounters a social world of which it is the product, it is like a 'fish in water': it does not feel the weight of the water, and it takes the world about itself for granted" (Bourdieu and Wacquant 1992: 127, quoted in Nkweto Simmonds 1997). When Bourdieu and Wacquant claim it is 'like a fish in water' when habitus come to encounter a social world of which it is the product, they as *white* males are forgetting that the relation racialized 'Others' have to this knowledge is conditioned. One is indeed at odds with the social world of which one is a product, for this world is *white*.

9 We were a group of young Black immigrant scholars and writers. I was the only one who stayed, but also the only one possessing a European passport; I had the privilege of Portuguese citizenship.

A few years later, I was still the only Black scholar in my colloquium, and then the only Black lecturer in my department, and one of the few in the whole institution. I cannot ignore how difficult it is to escape our body and its racist constructions within academia. While attending university, I remember being the only Black student at the department of Psychology, for five years. Among other things I learned about the pathology of the Black subject and that racism does not exist. At school, I remember *white* children sat in the front of the classroom, while the Black children sat in the back. We from the back were asked to write with the same words as those in the front – "because we are all equal," the teacher said. We were asked to read about the "Portuguese Discovery Epoch," even though we do not remember being discovered. We were asked to write about the great legacy of colonization, even though we could only remember robbery and humiliation. And we were asked not to inquire about our African heroes, for they were terrorists and rebels. What a better way to colonize than to teach the colonized to speak and write from the perspective of the colonizer. But, knowing that oppressed groups are frequently placed in the situation of being listened to only "if we frame our ideas in the language that is familiar to and comfortable for a dominant group" (Collins 2000: vii), I cannot escape the final question: How should I, as a Black woman, write within this arena? Patricia Hill Collins argues that the requirement that the oppressed be compelled to deliver a comfortable discourse often changes "the meaning of our ideal and works to elevate the ideas of dominant groups" (2000: vii). Thus comfort appears as a form of regulating marginalized discourses.[10] To whom should I write? And how should I write? Should I write against or for something? Sometimes writing turns into fear. I fear writing, for I hardly know if the words I am using are my salvation or my dishonor. It seems that everything surrounding me was, and still is, colonialism.

We had physicians, professors, statesmen. Yes, but something out of the ordinary still clung to such cases. 'We have a Senegalese history teacher. He is quite bright.... Our doctor is colored. He is very gentle.' It was always the Negro teacher, the Negro doctor; brittle as I was becom-

---

10 A good example of how scholarship can be regulated is described in *Outlaw Culture* by bell hooks (1994). hooks makes known how the Canadian government refused to allow her previous publication *Black Looks: Race and Representation* (1992) into Canada. They claimed the book was 'hate' literature and encouraged racial hatred. After massive protests the government finally released the book, suggesting there had been a misunderstanding, but the message that authorities are watching and ready to censor the discourses of the oppressed remains.

ing, I shivered at the slightest pretext. I knew, for instance, that if the physician made a mistake it would be the end of him and of all those who came after him. What could one expect, after all, from a Negro physician? As long as everything went well, he was praised to the skies, but look out, no nonsense, under any conditions! The black physician can never be sure how close he is to disgrace (Fanon 1967: 117).

Disgrace indeed, for one seems to be inside "the belly of the beast," says Stuart Hall. He uses this expression to describe the specific place and time from which he writes, as a Black intellectual. It is his position of enunciation. Born and raised in Jamaica, he lived all his adult life "in the shadow of the black diaspora" (Hall 1990: 223), inside the *beast*, a metaphor used to designate England. Being inside the beast announces somehow the place of danger from which he writes and theorizes – the danger of being from the margin and speaking at the centre.

THE MARGIN AND THE CENTRE

The margin and the centre that I am speaking of here, refer to the terms: *margin* and *centre*, as used by bell hooks. To be at the margin, she argues, is to be part of the whole but outside the main body. She recalls being part of a small Kentucky town where railroad tracks were daily reminders of her marginality, reminders that she was actually outside. Across those tracks was the centre: stores she could not enter, restaurants where she could not eat, and people she could not look directly in the face. It was a world where she could work as a maid, servant or prostitute, but not one where she could live; she always had to return to the margin. There were laws to ensure her return to the periphery, and severe punishments for those who would try to remain at the centre.

In this context of marginalization, she argues, Black women and Black men develop a particular way of seeing reality: both from the 'outside in' and from the 'inside out.' We focus our attention on both the centre as well as the margin because our survival depends on this awareness. Since the beginning of slavery, we have become experts of "psychoanalytic readings of the *white* Other" (hooks 1995: 31), and of how *white* supremacy is both structured and performed. In other words, we are experts on critical whiteness and postcolonialism.

In this sense, the margin should not only be seen as a peripheral space, a space of loss and deprivation, but rather a space of resistance and possibility.

It is a 'space of radical openness' (hooks 1989: 149) and creativity, where new critical discourses take place. It is here that oppressive boundaries set by 'race,' gender, sexuality and class domination are questioned, challenged and deconstructed. In this critical space, 'we can imagine questions that could not have been imagined before; we can ask questions that might not have been asked before' (Mirza 1997:4), questions that challenge the colonial authority of the centre and the hegemonic discourses within it. In this sense, the margin is a location that nourishes our capacity to resist oppression, to transform, and to imagine alternative new worlds and new discourses.

Speaking of the margin as a place of creativity can, of course, convey the danger of romanticizing oppression. To what extent are we idealizing peripheral positions and by doing so undermining the violence of the centre? However, bell hooks argues that this is not a romantic exercise, but the simple acknowledgment of the margin as a complex location that embodies more than one site. The margin is both a site of repression and a site of resistance (hooks 1990). Both sites are always present because *where there is oppression, there is resistance*; in other words, oppression forms the conditions for resistance.

A deep nihilism and destruction would penetrate us were we only to consider the margin a mark of ruin or speechlessness rather than a place of possibility. Stuart Hall, for instance, says that when he writes, he *writes against*. Writing against means speaking out against the silence and marginality created by racism. It is a metaphor that illustrates the struggle of colonized people to come into representation within dominant *white* regimes. One writes against in the sense that one opposes. bell hooks, however, argues that opposing or being 'against' is not enough. As I wrote in the introduction, one has to create new roles outside that colonial order. This is what Malcolm X once called the "decolonization of our minds and imaginations": learning to think and see everything with "new eyes," in order to enter the struggle as subjects and not as objects (quoted in hooks 1994: 7). This process of inventing oneself anew, argues bell hooks, emerges as one comes to understand how:

> structures of domination work in one's own life, as one develops critical thinking and critical consciousness, as one invents new alternative habits of being and resists from that marginal space of difference inwardly defined (hooks 1990: 15).

It is the understanding and the study of one's own marginality that creates the possibility of emanating as a new subject.

CHAPTER 3

SPEAKING THE UNSPEAKABLE

DEFINING RACISM

UNSPOKEN RACISM

Racism is a violent reality. It has been central to the making of European politics for centuries, starting with the European projects of slavery, colonization, and today's 'Fortress Europe.' Nevertheless, it is often seen as a peripheral phenomenon, marginal to the essential patterns of social and political lives, somehow "located at the surface of other things" (Gilroy 1992: 52), like a 'coat of paint' that can be easily scraped off. This image of a 'coat of paint' illustrates the prevalent fantasy that racism is 'something' on the structures of social relations, but not a determinant of those relations. Tendentiously, racism is seen as simply an external 'thing,' a 'thing' of the past, something located at the margins rather than at the center of European politics.

For many years, racism was neither seen nor reflected as a significant theoretical and practical problem in academic discourses, leading to a very serious theoretical deficit (Weiß 1998). On the one hand, this deficit emphasizes the low importance that has been given to the phenomenon of racism; on the other hand, it reveals the common disregard toward those who experience racism.

Most studies on racism have used what Philomena Essed calls a 'macro perspective' (1991); they are concerned with either the social and political structures of racism, or tendentiously concerned with the aggressor, as is the case with most research on racism conducted in Germany. Racist aggressors and members of right wing parties, writes Paul Mecheril (1998), must be quite satisfied with the extreme attention that both the media and scholarship have paid to them. There have been rows of books written and psychological trainings developed, as well as workshops, discussions and seminars, all in order to comprehend the aggressors. The actual victims of racism, however, have been rapidly forgotten. This disregard, or rather omission, mirrors the unimportance of Black people as political, social and individual subjects within European politics.

The experienced reality of racism, the subjective encounters, experiences, struggles, knowledge, understanding and feelings of Black people with respect to racism, as well as the psychic scars racism causes us, have been largely neglected (Essed 1990, 1991). These only become visible in public and academic spheres, when the normality of *white* national culture is suddenly disturbed, when our experiences with racism endanger the comfort of *white* society. At that moment, we and our reality with racism become visible, spoken and even written, not because we might be in danger or at risk, or need guardianship, but rather because such an uncomfortable reality disturbs *white* common immunity.

In most studies we become visible not through our own self-perception and self-determination, but rather through the perception and political interest of the dominant *white* national culture, as most studies and public debates on racism have "a white point of view" (Essed 1991: 7). We are, so to speak, fixed and measured from the outside by specific interests that satisfy the political criteria of the *white* subject, as largely discussed in the previous two chapters. Paul Mecheril (1997) illustrates this process of alienation in a humorous way, writing that while he reads the magazine *Spiegel*,[11] he has a great chance to learn about himself. The magazine informs him that immigrants and other kinds of foreigners[12] are a marginal group in Germany that operates as a collective time bomb to the nation. This terminology reflects the standpoint and the political interests of the dominant group toward the so-called 'Other Germans' – *die andere deutsche* – but not of the 'Other Germans' themselves. The metaphor of a ticking bomb denotes the emergent catastrophe immigrants seem to represent to the nation. It is this immediate calamity and the tragedy that each immigrant or *andere deutsche* imaginably embodies that place us at the very center of the magazine, on the cover, photo included. We become visible through the gaze and vocabulary of the *white* subject describing us: it is neither our words, nor our subjective voices printed on the pages of the magazine, but rather what we phantasmally represent to the *white* nation and its *real* nationals.

Contrary to this, I am concerned in this book with the subjective experiences of Black women with racism.

BECOMING THE SPEAKING SUBJECTS

To approach the experienced reality of racism within this context of massive disregard and objecthood, a shift in perspective is required, a shift into the so-called *subject's perspective* (Mecheril 1997: 37). In such a study the focus should not be on the construction of subjects as individuals, but rather the ways in which it is possible for individuals to act as subjects in their social realities, and – as this study deals exclusively with the testimonies of Black

---

11 A weekly German magazine dealing with current political and social items.

12 German citizens who have a heritage other than German are commonly classified as 'foreigners' – *Ausländer*.

women – the way in which it is possible for Black women to achieve the status of subjects in the context of gendered racism.

According to Paul Mecheril (2000), the idea of a subject, or at least the idealized concept of what a subject is, embodies three different levels: the *political*, the *social* and the *individual*. These compose the spheres of subjectivity. Ideally, people achieve the complete status of a subject when in their societal context they are acknowledged at all three different levels and when they identify and regard themselves acknowledged as such.

The term *subject* therefore specifies the relation an individual has with her/his society; it refers not to a substantial, but rather a relational concept. Having the status of subject means that on the one hand, individuals can find and present themselves in different spheres of inter-subjectivity and social realities and on the other hand, participate in their society; they can determine the topics and proclaim the themes and agendas of the society in which they live. In other words, they can see their own individual and collective interests officially recognized, validated and represented in society – the absolute status of a subject. Racism, however, violates each one of these spheres, as Black people and People of Color do not see their political, social and individual interests as part of the common agenda. So how does racism affect one's status of subjectivity?

DEFINING RACISM

Racism is attended by three simultaneous features: first, *the construction of difference*; one is seen as 'different' due to one's racial and/or religious belonging. Here, we have to ask: Who is 'different' from whom? Is the Black subject 'different' from the *white* subject, or the way around, the *white* 'different' from the Black? One only becomes 'different' because one 'differs' from a group who has the power to define itself as the norm – the *white* norm. All those who are not *white* are constructed as 'different,' and whiteness constructed as the reference point from which all racial 'Others' 'differ.' In this sense, one is not 'different,' one becomes 'different' through the process of discrimination.

Second, these constructed differences are *inseparably linked to hierarchical values*. Not only is the individual seen as 'different,' but also this difference is articulated through stigma, dishonor and inferiority. Such hierarchical values implicate a process of naturalization, as they are applied to all members of the same group who come to be seen as "the problematic," "the difficult," "the dangerous," "the lazy," "the exotic," "the colorful" and "the unusual." These two last processes – the construction of difference and its association with a hierarchy – form what is also called *prejudice*.

Finally, both processes are accompanied by *power* – historical, political, social and economical power. It is the combination of both prejudice and power that form racism. And in this sense, *racism is white supremacy*. Other racial groups can neither be racist nor perform racism, as they do not possess this power. The conflicts between them or between them and the *white* dominant group have to be organized under other definitions, such as prejudice. Racism instead includes the dimension of power and is revealed through global differences in the share of and access to valued resources such as political representation, policies, media, employment, education, housing, health, etc. Who can see their political interests represented in the national agendas? Who can see their realities portrayed in the media? Who can see their history included in educational programs? Who owns what? Who lives where? Who is protected and who is not?

Official and academic discourses in Germany have avoided using the term racism and instead use terms such as *Fremdfeindlichkeit* (enmity toward strangers) or *Ausländerfeindlichkeit* (enmity toward foreigners). These terms, however, are unsatisfactory because they do not explain that the central problem of racism is not the existence of diversity and diverse people, but rather the performed inequality between them. We are dealing here with a question of neither nationality (nationals or non-nationals),[13] nor sentiments (enmity or sympathy), but power.

STRUCTURAL RACISM

This is revealed at a structural level as Black people and People of Color are excluded from most social and political structures. Official structures operate in a way that manifestly privileges their *white* subjects, putting members of other racialized groups at a visible disadvantage, outside dominant structures. This is what is called *structural racism*.

---

13 The term 'Ausländerfeindlichkeit' constructs certain nationals as 'Ausländer,' and, in turn, as a unified group that experiences racism. It is, however, common sense that a *white* French or *white* Briton do not share the experience of racism with an Angolan or a Black Briton. Moreover, nationals such as Afro-Germans or Turkish-Germans do experience racism, but are not 'Ausländer.'

INSTITUTIONAL RACISM

As the term 'institution' implies, institutional racism emphasizes that racism is not only an ideological, but also an institutionalized phenomenon. It refers to a pattern of unequal treatment in everyday operations such as educational systems, educational agendas, labor markets, criminal justice, services, etc. Institutional racism operates in a way that puts *white* subjects at a clear advantage to other racialized groups.

EVERYDAY RACISM

Everyday racism refers to all vocabulary, discourses, images, gestures, actions and gazes that place the Black subject and People of Color not only as 'Other' – the difference against which the *white* subject is measured – but also as Otherness, that is, the personification of the aspects the *white* society has repressed.

Every time I am placed as 'Other' – whether it is the unwelcomed 'Other,' the intrusive 'Other,' the dangerous 'Other,' the violent 'Other,' the thrilling 'Other,' whether it is the dirty 'Other,' the exciting 'Other,' the wild 'Other,' the natural 'Other,' the desirable 'Other' or the exotic 'Other' – I am inevitably experiencing racism, for I am being forced to become the embodiment of what the *white* subject does not want to be acquainted with. I become the 'Other' of whiteness, not the self – and therefore I am being denied the right to exist as equal.

Within everyday racism one is used as a screen for projections of what the *white* society has made taboo. One becomes a deposit for *white* fears and fantasies from the realm of either aggression or sexuality. That is why in racism one can be perceived as 'intimidating' one minute and 'desirable' the next, and vice versa: 'fascinatingly attractive' at first, and afterward, 'hostile' and 'harsh.' In Freudian terms the two aspects of 'aggression' and 'sexuality' categorize the psychological organization of an individual. In *white* society, however, these two aspects of 'aggression' and 'sexuality' have been massively repressed and re-projected onto racial others. These processes of repression and projection allow the *white* subject to escape its historicity of oppression and construct itself as 'civilized' and 'decent,' while racial 'Others' become 'decivilized' (aggressive) and 'wild' (sexuality). One is perceived as either one or the other, taking the following forms:

Infantilization: The Black subject becomes the personification of the dependent – the boy, girl, child, or asexual servant – who cannot survive without the master.

Primitivization: The Black subject becomes the personification of the uncivilized – savage, backward, base, or natural – the one who is closer to nature.

Decivilization: The Black subject becomes the personification of the violent and threatening Other – the criminal, the suspect, the dangerous – the one who is outside of the law.

Animalization: The Black subject becomes the personification of the animal – the wild, the ape, the monkey, the 'King Kong' figure – another form of humanity.

Eroticization: The Black subject becomes the personification of the sexualized, with a violent sexual appetite: the prostitute, the pimp, the rapist, the erotic and the exotic.

Vocabulary, for instance, places me as 'Other' when on the news I hear them speaking about 'illegal immigrants.' Discourses place me as 'Other' when I am told that I cannot be from here because I am Black. Images place me as 'Other' when I walk down the street and find myself surrounded by advertisements with Black faces and compelling words like 'Help.' Gestures place me as 'Other' when at the bakery the *white* woman next to me tries to be attended to before me. Actions place me as 'Other' when I am monitored by the police as soon as I arrive at a central station. Gazes place me as 'Other' when people stare at me. Every time I am thus placed as 'Other,' I am experiencing racism, for I am not 'Other.' I am self.

The term 'everyday' refers to the fact that these experiences are not punctual. Everyday racism is not a 'single assault' or a 'discrete event,' but rather a 'constellation of life experiences,' a 'constant exposure to danger,' a 'continuing pattern of abuse' that repeats itself incessantly throughout one's biography – in the bus, at the supermarket, at a party, at a dinner, in the family.

DECIDING FOR SUBJECT-ORIENTED RESEARCH

Within racism we thus become incomplete subjects. Incomplete subjects are not equal to complete subjects; the latter "hold the power (...) to put into practice their own idea of superiority and their sense of being more deserving of certain rights and privileges" (Essed 1990: 10). Racism therefore functions to justify and legitimize the exclusion of racial 'Others' from certain rights. Those who speak in this book are 'incomplete subjects' in the sense that they are excluded from having certain spheres of subjectivity acknowledged: political, social and individual. This idealized understanding of 'subject' is echoed in this study at both empirical and theoretical levels. This work is a space to perform subjectivity, to acknowledge Black women in particular and Black people in general as subjects of this society – in all the real senses of the word.

Methodologically, this study seeks to understand, reconstruct and recover Black women's experiences with racism in a *white* patriarchal society, taking into account gender constructions and the impact of gender on forms and experiences of racism. For that purpose and considering the political and epistemological concerns mentioned earlier, I defend the need to guide my study as *subject-oriented research*[14] (Mecheril 1997, 2000), using biographical narrative interviews with Black women who recall their biographies within racism and through narratives of real-life experiences in Germany.

Subject-oriented research, as Paul Mecheril argues in his pioneering work on everyday racism (1997: 33), examines the experiences, self-perceptions and identity negotiations described by the subject and from the subject's perspective. One has the right to be a subject – a political, social and individual subject – and rather than the embodiment of Otherness, incarcerated in the realm of objecthood. This becomes conceivable only when one has the possibility of voicing one's own reality and experiences from one's own self-perception and definition, when one can (re)define and recover one's own history and reality. If Black women as well as other marginalized groups have the capital right, in all the senses of the term, to be acknowledged as subjects, then we should also have this right acknowledged within research processes and academic discourses. This method of focusing on the subject is not a privileged form of research, but a necessary concept.

All three forms of disregard – political, social and individual – are of high significance in the lives of Black people in *white* dominated societies because they real our reality. Moreover, they are reproduced in academic discourses through epistemologies and methods that place the voices of marginalized groups as secondary, depriving us of the right to self-representation. This, of course, reinforces the importance of conducting research *centered on the subject*, a so-called *study up* (Lofland & Lofland 1984 quoted in Essed 1991).

---

14 Translation of the original term *Subjektorientierte Untersuchung* (Mecheril 1997, 2000).

In a "study up" researchers investigate members of their own social group, or people of similar status, as a way of rectifying the constant reproduction of the status quo within knowledge production (Essed 1991, Mama 1995). Doing research among equals has been strongly encouraged by feminists, as it represents the ideal conditions for nonhierarchical relationships between the researchers and the informants: shared experiences, social equality and involvement with the problematic. For instance, it has been shown repeatedly that Black informants are reticent about discussing their experiences of racism with a *white* interviewer (Essed 191). The concept of 'study up' research complements the concept of 'subject-oriented' research described earlier, as both reject detachment from the 'research objects.' My position as a scholar is not of a detached subject looking at her 'researched objects,' but rather of 'conscious subjectivity' (Essed 1991: 67). This does not mean that I uncritically accept all the statements of the interviewees, but that I fully respect their accounts of racism and show genuine interest in the ordinary events of everyday life. This attitude of 'conscious subjectivity,' explains Philomena Essed, allows asking the interviewees to "qualify specific statements and to go into details without inducing defensive reactions from their side" (Essed 1991: 67). I therefore do not agree with the traditional point of view that emotional, social and political detachment is always a better condition for doing research than close involvement, as being an insider provides a rich base, valuable in subject-oriented research.

My choice of Black women of an age and class background similar to myself makes it possible to generate knowledge from more egalitarian power relations between researcher and researched.

THE INTERVIEWEES

Two similar groups of women were interviewed: 3 Afro-Germans and 3 women of African descent living in Germany, a Ghanaian, an Afro-Brazilian and an African-American. The selection was based not on nationality, but rather on the fact that all of the women, just like myself, were Black; they were African or African Diasporic women living in Germany.

To find the interviewees I wrote a short announcement referring to my research project in German, English and Portuguese (my mother language). I used three criteria: (1) I sent the announcement to several African and/or African Diasporic organizations, cultural institutes, student groups, etc.; (2) I used references through my personal contacts and (3) references through my professional contacts. Interviewees were requested to be between the ages of 25 and 45. Thus diversity was obtained in different ways.

After conducting all of the interviews, I chose to analyze only two of them: the interviews with Alicia, an Afro-German (33) woman, and Kathleen, an African-American (27) woman living in Germany, for the simple fact that both offered very rich and varied information about the experienced reality of racism. Even though the other four women delivered important information about everyday racism, their narratives were not as rich and diverse as those of Alicia and Kathleen. In order to avoid repetitive material, I decided instead to work intensely with only two of the six interviews as they revealed such vast information about everyday racism.

While the other four interviewees offered somewhat intervallic and infrequent material, Alicia and Kathleen delivered continuous and continuous material on everyday racism, making it possible to use a whole interview as data. Their interviews covered both the subject matter given by the other interviewees as well as additional themes. Moreover, as Kathleen was at the time actively involved in a project about creative forms of dealing with Black isolation in a *white* setting, she also appeared an expert, contributing immensely to the analysis of everyday racism.

THE INTERVIEW

For the empirical research, I used *nondirective* interviews based on *biographical narratives*. The *biographical narrative* approach allows not only for learning about the interviewees' current experiences of racism, but allows interviewees to create a *gestalt* about the reality of racism in their lives. This permits the reconstruction of the Black experience within racism.

It is extremely important to have this biographical perspective when working with the phenomenon of racism because the experience of racism is not a momentary or punctual act, but rather a continuous experience throughout one's biography, an experience that involves a historical memory of racial oppression, slavery, and colonization.

The *nondirective* interview permits the interviewer to encourage the interviewees to talk about a given topic with a minimum of direct questioning or guidance. In this sense, the interviewees have the chance to speak freely about their experiences of racism and to make free associations between those experiences and other issues which they define as relevant to their experiences with racism (Essed 1991). For example, during the interviews, two of the women spoke of their mothers' suicides and related them to racism, while a third spoke of a girl-friend's suicide. Through free association we come to understand that suicide was, from the perspective of these interviewees, related to the experience of racism – a result of their friend's and mothers' invisibility and exclusion. The fact that suicide is so overly present in these different African Diaspora biographies gives rise as well to a new perspective about what it is to experience racism.

Thus the nondirective biographical narrative interview permits the interviewees to define their subjective reality and experience of racism in their lives. This does not mean that I as scholar do not have any control over the general structure of the interview, then, I use a minimal global interview schema. The interview schedule was based on the main clusters of information I wished to study[15]:

(i) perceptions of racial identity and racism in childhood
(ii) general perceptions of racism and racial issues in the family
(iii) personal and vicarious experiences of racism in everyday life
(iv) perceptions of self in relation to other Blacks
(v) perceptions of whiteness in the Black imaginary
(vi) perceptions of Black female beauty and hair matters
(vii) perceptions of Black femininity
(viii) the sexualization of Black Women.

The interviews lasted three to three and half hours. One could probably get more data from longer interviews, but it would not be realistic to process so much information in one project. Moreover, as I mentioned earlier, a long series of interviews would not produce a complete reconstruction of the reality of everyday racism in the life of an individual Black woman in this society. Another advantage of only one interview per interviewee was that I could work with spontaneous accounts and also avoid the usual variations and repetition in stories.

The interviews were conducted in English, German and Portuguese, according to the interviewees' choice. It was important to me that the interviewees have the chance to speak in a language they felt comfortable with, so not to articulate their very personal experiences in a language of discomfort. Most of the interviews took place in my private home.

---

15 In this study interpretations of racism are reconstructed through the analysis of accounts gathered in nondirective interviews.

ANALYSIS

There is no normative model that describes the ideal steps involved in analyzing data about everyday racism (Essed 1991). I therefore did not sample extracts in accordance with a predefined sampling technique. Instead, I chose to transcribe each interview and subsequently select episodes based on central topics of experiences of everyday racism as told by the interviewees through their biographies. I call this form of analysis: *episodic*.

Everyday racism occurs in a particular context; it is aimed at particular goals and involves particular actors or social conditions. An episodic analysis describes the different contexts in which racism is being performed, creating a sequence of scenes of everyday racism. The composition of several episodes reveals not only the complexity of experiencing of racism – its different scenarios, actors and themes – but also its uninterrupted presence in one's own life. This form of episodic analysis also allows me to write in a new style similar to short stories, which, as described earlier, transgresses traditional scholarship.

I divided the interviews into episodes and for each selected episode used a title that revealed the context and content of racism. All the titles consist of a quotation from the interviewee's narrative and are sometimes followed by a sub-title that helps to identify the theoretical problem. For example, in: *"(...) they want to hear an exotic story" – voyeurism and Otherness*, the title quotation is about how the interviewee is often asked to tell a story that places her outside the German nation as the pleasurable and exotic 'Other,' while the sub-title indicates the theoretical themes. In this sense, the titles reveal both what the interviewees define as everyday racism as well as its theoretical content.

In the tradition of Fanon's writings and of other Black scholars such as bell hooks, I have opted for a phenomenological interpretation instead of an abstract one. In this work, for instance, I am not concerned with abstracting what voyeurism or desire is, but rather with describing the phenomenon itself: how is desire being performed in the scene? And how is desire experienced by the subject who is speaking? What seems to be the function of desire in the realm of everyday racism? Like an attentive observer I describe the phenomenon in detail, but do not necessarily abstract it. Abstracting is, of course, a very important dimension of knowledge production; in this work, however, deciding to abstract the subjective experiences of everyday racism could be problematic in that it imposes terminology upon experience, and objectivity upon subjectivity. Abstracting the subjective accounts of Black women can easily become a form of silencing their voices in order to objectify them under universal terminologies. This would not produce subjectivity, but would instead reproduce a dominant form of knowledge production. For this reason, I opted consciously to analyze the interviews at a phenomenological level.

I see this not as a deficit, but as a form of interpretation that gives space to new language and new discourse, and that is concerned with the production of subjectivity rather than the production of universal knowledge. "I am not a potentiality of something," writes Fanon, "I am wholly what I am. I do not have to look for the universal" (1967: 135). While traditionally the *white* subject would write: "I am a potentiality of something, I am not wholly what I am. I do have to look for the universal" – I have been everywhere and touched everything. In opposition to *white* dominant scholarship, Fanon does not see himself as the embodiment of the absolute, of the powerful. As a Black man he is not searching for the universal; he simply describes what he sees. In his writings he invites us into his universe, not into the universal, and this subjectivity is an important dimension of marginal discourses and a creative form of decolonizing knowledge. When opting for a phenomenological interpretation, I believe I am transforming again configurations of both knowledge and power.

The interview chapters consist of an interpretative analysis based on psychoanalytical and postcolonial theory. I thus create a dialogue between Fanon's psychoanalytical theory and postcolonialism. More specifically, this study embraces the psychoanalytical theory of Frantz Fanon on colonialism and racism, providing a systematic framework for the analysis of everyday traumas and the psychic costs of racial inequality at the level of subjectivity. Moreover, Fanon's psychoanalytical theory is deeply concerned with racial and sexual difference within a colonial schema, providing important insight into the analysis of data. For various reasons, postcolonial theory offers the appropriate framework for the analysis of 'race' and gender politics, colonial politics and the political strategies of decolonization. Both approaches become complementary for the understanding of the individual and collective experiences of Black women within racism.

I argue that it is worth looking at individual experiences and subjective accounts of everyday racism in order to understand the collective and historical memory. As Philomena Essed emphasizes, analyzing experiences of everyday racism is putting systematic links between interpretations of subjective experiences and the organization of categories concerning racism. This means that "characteristics of the interviews are seen as (preliminary) indications of the definition and attributive explanations of everyday racism" (Essed 1991: 69).

My decision on what data was relevant for specific experiences or events was based on both the interviewees' definition and a comparison of characteristics of the event with other relevant cases. This was to increase the probability that a certain event was an example of everyday racism. Judgments about specific experiences or events were usually based on two types of judgmental heuristics: drawing on prior theories or expectations about racism and racial issues, and comparing characteristics of the event with other relevant cases to assess the probability that a certain event was an example of racism.

The purpose of the analysis was to identify the following information in the interview materials:

(i) space politics

(ii) hair politics

(iii) sexual politics

(iv) skin politics

(v) psychological scars imposed by everyday racism

(vi) psychological strategies for healing from and/or overcoming everyday racism

(vii) resistance strategies

CHAPTER 4

GENDERED RACISM

"(...) WOULD YOU LIKE TO CLEAN OUR HOUSE?" – CONNECTING 'RACE' AND GENDER

"(...) WOULD YOU LIKE TO CLEAN OUR HOUSE?"

When I was about twelve or thirteen years old, I went to the doctor because I had the flu. After the consultation, as I was turning toward the door, he suddenly called me back. He had been looking at me, he said, and had had an idea. He and his wife and two children, who were around eighteen and twenty-one years old, were going on holiday. They had rented a house in the South of Portugal, somewhere in Algarve, and he was thinking that I could come with them. He proposed that I cook their daily meals, clean their house and eventually wash their clothes: "It's not much," he said, "some shorts, sometimes a T-shirt, and, of course, our underwear!" Between these tasks, he explained, I would have enough free time for myself. I could go to the beach, "and do whatever you want," he insisted. He had African masks decorating the other side of the office, I must have looked at them. "They are from Guinea Bissau!" he said. "I was working there... as a doctor!" I looked at him, silent. I do not actually remember if I was able to say anything. I don't think I was. But I do recall leaving the office in a state of dizziness and vomiting some streets further, before arriving home. *I was up against something unreasoned.*

In this scenario, the young girl is not seen as a child, but rather as a servant. The man transformed our doctor/patient relationship into a master/servant relationship: from patient I turn into the Black servant, just like him from doctor turns into a symbolic *white* master, a double construction, both outside and inside. In these binary constructions the dimension of power between the oppositions are twice inverted. It is not only a question of, 'Black patient, *white* doctor,' or, 'female patient, male doctor,' but of 'Black female patient, *white* male doctor' – power double for one another and "play across the structures of otherness, complicating its politics" (Hall 1992: 256). It seems that we are stuck in a theoretical dilemma: is this racism or sexism?

One could place the problem of underestimation in the context of gender, since I – a girl – was being asked to become the domestic worker of an adult male, after a medical consultation. This scene, however, takes place within the realm of both racial and gender differences, for the doctor is not just male; he is a *white* male and I am not only a girl, but a Black girl.

This encounter reveals how 'race' and gender are inseparable. 'Race' can neither be separated from gender nor gender from 'race.' The experience involves both because racist constructions are based on gender roles and vice-versa, and gender has an impact on the construction of 'race' and the experience of racism. The myth of the disposable Black woman, the infantilized Black man, the oppressed Muslim woman, the aggressive Muslim man, as well as the myth of the emancipated *white* woman or the liberal *white* man, are examples of how gender and 'race' constructions interact.

Analytically it is difficult to determine in detail the specific impact of either 'race' or gender because they are always interlocked. But what would happen if we would change the 'race' and gender of the characters? What if this scenario had comprised a *white* man and a *white* girl? Would he have asked her to serve him and his family? Would he have looked upon the *white* girl as a servant? Or rather as a child?

And if the accent were on gender, then how come the wife, a female like me, could 'own' me as a servant and not be a servant herself? If as females we are equals, how is it that she could become my virtual mistress and I the figurative slave? How much would her absenteeism play an active role in my servitude? What about the daughter, who is referred to during the proposal, how is it that she is older but protected as a child while the Black girl is much younger, but exploited as an adult? Is it not that the emancipation of both the *white* wife and *white* daughter comes at the expense of the Black girl, who is asked to serve them for free?

What if the doctor had been a Black male, would he have asked a *white* girl, his patient, to become his servant during his holidays? Would he have asked her to cook for him and his family and wash their clothes while they played on the beach? Or the other way around: Had the doctor been a Black woman, would she have asked a *white* girl to work for her and her household? Would she have insisted that the *white* girl join her family in order to serve? Could such a colonial fantasy take place in the office of a Black physician? And had there been a *white* female doctor and a Black boy as the patient, would it have been possible that at the end of the consultation he would have been asked by the *white* woman to serve her? Very possibly.

Even though there is a complex intersection between 'race' and gender, changing the 'race' of the characters, more than changing gender, would profoundly shift the set of power relations. All *white* characters would have remained protected, but none of the Black characters. It might therefore be assumed that many, if not the majority, of personal experiences of racism, which are forms of 'gendered racism' (Essed 1991: 5). In this chapter I intend to explore the connections between 'race,' gender and racism. In other words, I will conceptualize gendered racism.

BLACK MALE vs. *WHITE* FEMALE AND BLACK WOMEN'S ABSENCE

Most of the literature on racism has failed to address the specific position of Black women and the way matters of gender and sexuality relate to matters of 'race.' Racism has conditioned Black people in such a way that 'race' often becomes regarded "as the only relevant aspect of our lives and gender oppression as insignificant in light of the harsher, more atrocious reality of racism" (hooks 1981: 1). A great deal of Black politics has constructed its subjects around conceptions of Black heterosexual masculinity. The construction of the Black subject as 'masculine' is problematic because it renders invisible Black female and gay/queer experiences. This conceptualization simply turns the classic concept '*white* male heterosexual' into 'Black male heterosexual,' being 'race' the only changed category. In this sense, Black female and Black gay/queer scholars have, in recent years, questioned this conceptualization, crossing racism with questions of gender and sexuality in what has been called the 'new politics of representation' (Hall 1992) or 'new cultural politics of difference' (West 1995). However, Western feminist literature has also failed to acknowledge that gender affects women from other racialized groups differently than it does *whites*, making Black women invisible. In Western feminist discourses the dominant concept of '*white* male heterosexual' has become '*white* female heterosexual.' A single category has changed in opposition to its inverse from male to female, maintaining its conservative racial structure: *white*.

DEFINING GENDERED RACISM

Black women have thus been positioned within several discourses that misrepresent our own reality: a debate on racism where the subject is Black male; a gendered discourse where the subject is *white* female; and a discourse on class where 'race' has no place at all. We occupy a very critical place within theory.

It is because of this ideological lack, argues Heidi Safia Mirza (1997) that Black women inhabit an empty space, a space that overlaps the margins of 'race' and gender, the so-called 'third space.' We inhabit a kind of vacuum of erasure and contradiction "sustained by the polarization of the world into Blacks on one side and women on the other" (Mirza 1997: 4). Us in between. This is, of course, a serious theoretical dilemma, in which the concepts of 'race' and gender narrowly merge into one. Such separate narratives maintain the invisibility of Black women in academic and political debates.

The Black female reality, however, is a hybrid phenomenon, as Philomena Essed (1991) argues. A phenomenon that crosses several conceptions of 'race' and gender, our reality can only be adequately approached when these respective concepts are taken into account. In order to include both categories, some authors, such as Joe Feagin and Yanick St. Jean (1998) have spoken of a 'Double Burden' to describe the reality of Black women and 'race' and gender. Other authors speak of a 'triple burden' to designate Black women's position in society (Westwood 1984 quoted in Anthias & Yuval-Davis), in the sense that Black women experience racism, sexism and/or homophobia – positioning us in a double or even triple dimension.

These terms, however, are insufficient because they treat different forms of oppression – such as racism, sexism and homophobia – as cumulative rather than intersecting. The intersection of forms of oppression cannot be seen as a simple increase of layers, but instead as the "production of specific effects" (Anthias & Yuval-Davy 1992: 100). Forms of oppression do not operate in singularity; they intersect with others. Racism, for instance, does not function as a distinct ideology and structure; it interacts with other ideologies and structures of domination such as sexism (Essed 1991, hooks 1989).

In this sense, the simultaneous impact of 'race' and gender oppression leads to forms of racism that are unique to the experiences of Black women and women of color. Their manifestations, explains Philomena Essed, overlap some forms of sexism against *white* women and racism against Black men. It is therefore useful to speak of *gendered racism* (Essed 1991: 30) to refer to the racial oppression of Black women as structured by racist perceptions of gender roles.

RACISM vs. SEXISM

Because many contemporary debates have posed the relation between 'race' and gender as parallel, there is a tendency to equate sexism and racism. *White* feminists have irresistibly tried to make analogies between their experiences with sexism and Black people's experiences with racism, reducing both to a similar form of oppression. These attempts often emerge in sentences like: "As a woman, I can understand what racism is" or "as a woman, I am discriminated against, just as Blacks are." In such sentences whiteness is not named, and it is exactly this no-naming of whiteness that allows *white* women to compare themselves to Black people in general and, at the same time, ignore the fact that Black women are also gendered – rendering Black women invisible.

It can, of course, be argued that as processes, racism and sexism are similar because ideologically they both construct common sense through reference to 'natural' and 'biological' differences. However, we cannot mechanistically understand gender and racial oppression as parallel because they affect and position groups of people differently, and, in the case of Black women, they interlock. In the attempt to compare sexism and racism, *white* feminists forget to conceptualize two crucial points: first, that they are *white* and therefore have *white* privileges, making it impossible to compare their experiences to the experiences of Black people, both female and male; and second, that Black women are also female and therefore also experience sexism. An ironic, but tragic, failure that has made Black women invisible voices within the global feminist project.

THE FALSE IDEA OF UNIVERSAL *SISTERHOOD*

Western feminists were, and are, keen on the idea of women's *Sisterhood*. The term speaks to a universalism among women. They conceptualize women as a collective, gendered, oppressed group in a patriarchal society. The term 'sisterhood' assumes the belief of a familiar link among all women of the world – the sisters – and a longing for female complicity within a male dominated world. When contextualized, this idea can be quite powerful; when not, it remains a false and simplistic assumption that neglects the history of slavery, colonialism and racism in which *white* women have been offered a share of *white* male power in relation to both Black women and men.

This model of a world divided into powerful men and subordinate women has been strongly criticized by Black feminists, first, because it neglects racist power structures among different women; second, because it cannot explain why Black men don't profit from patriarchy; third, because it does not take into account that, owing to racism, the way gender is constructed for Black women differs from constructions of *white* femininity; and finally, because this model implies a universalism among women that places gender as a primary and unique focus of attention, and, since 'race' and racism are not being addressed, relegates Black women to invisibility.

To acknowledge Black women's reality, we have to recognize the interlocking of 'race' and gender in structures of identification. The inappropriateness of the term 'sisterhood' becomes obvious in the episode I recalled at the beginning of this chapter, as it cannot explain why a Black girl is being asked to become the servant of a *white* woman and her *white* daughter. In this scene, there is no 'sisterhood,' and no complicity between the three women, but rather a hierarchy – a racial hierarchy, since I was being asked to become the servant of *white* women.

In general, *white* women are extraordinarily reluctant to see themselves as oppressors, as Hazel Carby writes, the involvement of *white* women:

> in imperialism and colonialism is repressed and the benefits that they – as whites – gained from the oppression of black people ignored. (...) The benefits of a white skin did not just apply to a handful of cotton, tea or sugar plantation mistresses; all women (...) benefited – in varying degrees – from the economic exploitation of the colonies (Carby 1997: 49).

Black feminists therefore speak of a false universality because women are being defined with reference to a *white* notion of womanhood, denying Black women a voice (Collins 2000; Fulani 1988; hooks 1992; Mirza 1997). In this false universalism the reality, concerns and claims of Black women become specific and illegitimate, while the experiences of *white* women prevail as universal, suitable and legitimate. As it is often argued by *white* feminists: feminism is about sexism, not racism.

'RACE' vs. GENDER

As I mentioned earlier, this failure to recognize the intersection between 'race,' gender and racial power structures renders Black women invisible within feminist theorizations. Black feminists still continue to demand that the existence of racism be acknowledged as a structuring feature (hooks 1981). There has been, however, strong resistance within Western feminist discourses to accepting and theorizing racism as a crucial and central dimension of the female experience. Afro-German feminists, for instance, have claimed this theoretical view in the German context for more than twenty years. Since the beginning of the 1980s, Afro-German feminists and writers such as Katharina Oguntoye and May Ayim (1986) have been writing and theorizing a Black female perspective in feminism. Yet, their work has often been ignored and placed outside the German academic context. Only recently have some *white* feminists started to reflect these aspects in their theoretical work, but it has been far from satisfying. By conceptualizing gender as the only starting point of oppression, feminist theories ignore the fact that Black women are not only oppressed by men – both *white* and Black – and institutionalized forms of sexism, but also by racism – from both *white* men and *white* women – and institutionalized forms thereof.

The anti-racist struggle was not of concern to Western feminism, primarily because their *white* initiators were and are not confronted with the violence of racism, but 'only' with sexualized oppression. Gender thus became the unique focus of their theories. *White* feminists have been particularly concerned with Black women's genitals and sexuality – such as genital mutilation and motherhood – on the one hand because their experiences of oppression as females focus on sexual violence, and on the other hand owing to *white* colonial fantasies about participating in the controlling of Black women's genitals, bodies and sexuality.

The dominant feminist paradigm, writes Jane Gaines, "actually encourages us not to think in any terms of oppression other than male dominance and female subordination" (2001: 403), neglecting racism as a subject in feminist theories – an immense failure for a social movement that is concerned with the ways in which women have been oppressed.

Ignoring 'race' and failing to take a strong stance against racism, argue Anthias and Yuval-Davis, "are seen [by Black feminists] as the products of the endemic racism of *White* feminism" (1992: 101). Such failure replicates racism. *White* feminists were interested in reflecting upon oppression as subordinate members of a patriarchy, but not upon their position as *whites* in a *white* supremacist society – in other words, a group in power in a racist structure. This model of men versus women obscures the function of 'race' and places *white* woman outside racist structures, saving them from acknowledging responsibility for racism and/or seeing themselves as practicing racism toward other groups of women [and men]. This again leads to a theoretical inadequacy in feminist theories. As bell hooks writes:

(s)exist discrimination has prevented *white* women from assuming the dominant role in the perpetuation of *white* racial imperialism, but it has not prevented *white* women from absorbing, supporting, and advocating racist ideology or acting individually as racist oppressors (hooks 1981: 124)

PATRIARCHY vs. *WHITE* PATRIARCHY

The model of absolute patriarchy was questioned by Black feminists and redefined in a more complex concept that would include 'race,' as "racism ensures that Black men do not have the same relations to patriarchal/capitalist hierarchies as *white* men" (Carby 1997: 46). Most authors therefore speak of '*white* patriarchy' (hooks 1981, 1995; Collins 2000) or 'racial patriarchy' to emphasize the importance of 'race' in gender relations.

Furthermore, to apply the classic notion of patriarchy to various colonial situations is equally unsatisfactory because it cannot explain why Black males have not enjoyed the benefits of *white* patriarchy. There are very obvious power structures in both colonial and slave formation and they are predominantly patriarchal, writes Carby; "(h)owever, the historically specific forms of racism force us to modify or alter the application of the term 'patriarchy' to Black men" (1997: 48). The notion of *white* patriarchy, she continues, has provided a convenient scapegoat for Black males, since "Black women have been dominated 'patriarchally' in different ways by men of different 'colours'" (Carby 1997: 48). Black men, writes bell hooks, "could join with *white* and black women to protest against *white* male oppression and divert attention away from their sexism, their support of patriarchy, and their sexist exploitation of women" (1981: 87-8). Still, the patriarchal system in the realm of racial difference is more complex, as is the position of Black males and females within racial patriarchy.

At this point, Black feminists diverge from *white* feminists, insisting that they do not necessarily see Black males as patriarchal antagonists, but instead feel that their racial oppression is 'shared' with men. This obviously suggests a new definition of patriarchy that includes the complex structures of 'race' and gender. It furthermore suggests a new perspective for feminism by claiming that Black women might want to organize themselves around racism using the category of gender. If Black feminists hesitate to emphasize gender as a category, it is in defense of the way Black women narrate their experience, for it is clear that Black women have historically formulated identity and political allegiance in terms of 'race' rather than gender or class, as "they experience oppression first in relation to 'race' rather than gender" (Gaines 2001: 403).

As Barbara Smith writes:

> Our situation as Black people necessitates that we have solidarity
> around the fact of race, which *white* women of course do not need

to have with *white* men, unless it is their negative solidarity as racial oppressors. We struggle together with Black men against racism, while we struggle with Black men about sexism (Smith 1983: 275)

The dialogue about the impact of sexism on Black women has been largely silenced in Black communities, as bell hooks (1981) explains, not only as a direct response against *white* women liberationists or as gesture of solidarity with Black males – but also as the silence of the oppressed. The struggle against racism, she writes, had conditioned Black women to devalue their femaleness and to regard 'race' as the only relevant category. "We were afraid to acknowledge that sexism could be just as oppressive as racism" (hooks 1981: 1).

DECOLONIZING BLACK WOMEN

The invisibility of Black women exposes this separate dialogue. In her essay *fantasizing Black women in Black Skin, White Masks,* Lola Young (1996) explores the terms in which Black women are discussed in the texts of Frantz Fanon. Fanon, who describes the psychological effects of colonialism and racism, systematically uses the term 'man' to designate its subjects, ignoring the specific experience of women in the context of racism. Lola Young argues that masculine terminology has been adjusted to explain the reality of all those who experience racism because 'man' appears as synonymous with 'people.'

In his writing Fanon uses the term 'man' to designate both 'Black man' and 'human being' – and also sometimes to designate himself, 'Frantz Fanon.' Hommi Bhabha argues that when the author says 'man,' he "connotes a phenomenological quality of humanness inclusive of man and woman" (1986: xxvi). The use of masculine terms to designate people-hood automatically reduces the existence of women to non-existence. "Are Black women in or out of the frame in Fanon's statement which begins 'The Black is a Black man...'? In or out of the frame when Fanon asks, 'What does a Black man want?'" (Young 1996: 88). In question is not simply the sexist use of a generic pronoun, she argues, but a matter of the ontological status of Black women. She thus speaks of Black women as 'missing persons' in the debate, those who do not own designation and who vanish within a major group: "(T)hose who have little or no power are so categorized not just because they have nothing but because they are nothing; they are excluded because they are considered to be nothing" (Young 1996: 88).

The claim of Black feminists is not to rank the structures of oppression in such a way that Black women have to choose between solidarity with Black men or with *white* women, between 'race' or gender, but instead to make our reality and experience visible in both theory and history. Black women's movements and theory have in this sense had a central role in the development of a postmodernist critique, offering a new perspective to contemporary debates on gender and postcolonialism.

In this work, however, we are not 'missing persons,' but rather 'speaking persons,' speaking subjects who are transforming theory. That Black women are affected by multiple forms of oppression – racism, sexism and/or homophobia – and that the foregoing discussion on racism and feminism has revealed the almost complete absence of Black women from consideration in both fields – these alone make the study of Black women a worthwhile enterprise. Just as in studies of other hitherto unconsidered groups, studies of and with Black women are likely to generate material that has implications both for the ways in which 'race' and gender have so far been theorized and for social theory in general.

CHAPTER 5

SPACE POLITICS

1. "WHERE DO YOU COME FROM?" – BEING PLACED OUTSIDE THE NATION

> People always asked me where do I come from: "Where do you come from?" And that was the thing... they asked me again and again and again... since I was a child, just like that! They see you and the first thing that crosses their mind is to check: "Where is she from?" They just walk in your direction and ask, without even knowing you. It does not matter where you are at: in a bus, at a party, on the street, a dinner or even at the supermarket (...) That is so racist, because they know there are Black people who are German and who even speak German better than them.

These are the words of Alicia, an Afro-German woman. From very early on, *white* people living around her have confronted her with questions concerning her body and her national origins, reminding her that she cannot be 'German' because she is Black. This constant questioning about where she comes from is not only an exercise of curiosity or of interest, but also an exercise in confirming dominant fantasies around 'race' and territoriality. Alicia is being asked in the first place because she is categorized as a 'race' that 'does not belong' (Essed, 1991).

The question contains the colonial fantasy that 'German' means *white* and Black means stranger (*Fremdl er*) or foreigner (*Ausländer*). It is a construction in which 'race' is imagined within specific national boundaries, and nationality in terms of 'race.' Both *Blackness* and *German-ness* (or *European-ness*) are reproduced here as two contradictory categories that mutually exclude each other. One is either Black *or* German, but not Black *and* German; the '*and*' is replaced by '*or*,' making Blackness incompatible with German-ness. As Alicia explains, this misconstruction makes the question of where she comes from "so racist," because "they know there are Black people who are German."

It is precisely this incompatibility between 'race' and nationality that defines *new forms of racism* (Gilroy 1987).[16] While *old* forms of racism appealed for 'biological races' and the idea of 'superiority' versus 'inferiority'

---

16 The term *new racism* makes a clear distinction between the old 'scientific racism' of the nineteenth and early twentieth centuries, and the racism of the late twentieth and twenty-first centuries. Such terminology emphasizes that racism is not a static and singular phenomenon; it exists in plural forms and, like any other social phenomenon, it is in a state of constant change.

– and the exclusion of those who were 'inferior' – *new* forms of racism rarely make reference to 'racial inferiority,' speaking instead of 'cultural difference' or 'religions' and their incompatibility with the national culture.[17] Racism has therefore changed its vocabulary. We have moved from the concept of 'biology' to the concept of 'culture,' and from the idea of 'hierarchy' to the idea of 'difference.'

Within contemporary racisms there is no place for 'difference.' Those who are 'different' remain perpetually incompatible with the nation; they can never actually belong, they are irreconcilably *Ausländer*. "Where do you come from?" "Why are you here?" "When do you intend to go back?" These questions embody exactly this fantasy of incompatibility. At first glance, the idea of superiority does not seem to be implied in new racisms, only the inoffensive thought that: "we have nothing against them, but those who are 'different' have their own countries to live in, and therefore they should return" as "their presence is a disturbance to the nation's integrity." Racism is thus explained in terms of 'territoriality,' assuming an almost natural feature. The repetitive enquiry illustrates the *white* desire to make Alicia irreconcilable with the nation; whenever she is asked, she is being denied authentic national membership on the basis of 'race.' The question unveil the *white* subject's reluctance to accept that it is not that *we do have our own countries to live in* but rather that *we are living in our country*.

I cannot help remembering how the street where I grew up in Lisbon, Portugal, officially named *rua Dr. João de Barros*,[18] became known as *rua dos Macacos* – 'The Monkeys' street.' Sometimes it was called 'República das Bananas,' an imaginary nation inhabited by monkeys. In the eyes of *whites*, we, the Blacks, were 'monkeys' who had recently arrived from formerly colonized Africa.[19] On the one hand, the grotesque fantasy of classifying

---

17 The term *new racism* was first used by Martin Barker (1981) after analyzing the discourses of British Conservative politicians and other right-wing thinkers. Despite the evident racist tonality of their speeches, these conservatives never made reference to 'race'; instead, they talked about *difference* and the impossibility of living with people who are 'culturally different,' and appealed for the repatriation of such people in order to maintain a *pure* British nation (Barker 1981, Rattansi 1994).

18 The name of a well-known Portuguese doctor.

19 The two-kilometer long street was the first road to which Black people moved; the *white* population later left its surrounding streets and new Black neighbors moved in, very soon turning the area into a majority African neighborhood. In my neighborhood – Mercês – most people were from the São Tomé e Príncipe, Angolan and Mozambique diasporas, as well as Roma and Sinti, who had been taken from the central city areas

us as monkeys, reveal the need to assert our position as inferior – outside humanity. On the other hand, the need to imagine our street as an illusory separate country reveals this forced incompatibility of Blackness and Portugueseness. They wanted indeed to imagine us living in another country, not there, but outside, in our own Republic. Twice. Doubly excluded. Doubly placed as 'Other.' So every time we left our republic or *ghetto*[20], we were asked, "Where do you come from?" As a reminder of where we should be.

2. "(...) BUT YOU CANNOT BE GERMAN." – COLONIAL FANTASIES AND ISOLATION

And if I answer and say that I am German, they look confused, you know? They stop for a moment, like thinking: "German...?" Or they just start laughing, as if I misunderstood the question or gave the wrong answer, you know? And they go: "Oh! No, no! But you cannot be German. You don't look German (*pointing to the skin*). Where are you from?"

Being looked at and questioned are forms of control that of course embody power. Alicia is looked at – the "'race' in the field of vision" (Hall 1996) – and questioned because she is expected to justify her presence in *white* territory.

Those who question exercise a power relation that defines Alicia's presence as *Fremde* (stranger) and the territory as theirs, drawing a clear boundary between You, the racial 'Other,' who is being questioned and has to explain, and We, the *whites*, who question and control. This power asymmetry, common of *whites* in relation to Blacks, reminds me of an old and painful slave/master relationship: Alicia is being asked and not doing the asking because it is the 'slave' who has to reply and the 'master' who controls. Sometimes *white* people say that when they were on holidays, they too were asked where

---

and moved to the suburbs where the African communities were living. North of my neighborhood were people of the Cabo-Verdian and Guinea Bissau diasporas, and South, people of the East Timor diaspora.

20 The term *ghetto* is derived from the Jewish diaspora. Ghetto is the name of the island in front of Venice, Italy, where in 1516, Italian Jews were deported after being prohibited from living on the continent among the dominant national culture. The term *ghetto* was later adopted by other Diasporic people, such as Africans, to describe our experiences of exclusion and Apartheid (Jelloun 1998).

they are from, trying to equalize both experiences. These however cannot be equalized, for even when the colonized asks, it is colonizer who has the power. This explains why the question is so disturbing when posed by *white* subjects, but not when posed by other Black people or People of Color.

The expectation that racial 'Others' tell their origins and expose their biographies '*in the bus, at a party, on the street, a dinner or even at the supermarket*' unveils a colonial dialectic in which the *white* subject presents itself as the absolute authority, the master, while the Black subject is forced into subordination. One suddenly becomes an object for *white* others to look at, address and question, at any time and any place. While the *white* subject is occupied with the question "what do I see?" the Black subject is forced to deal with the question "what do they see?"

Sometimes Alicia answers that she is German, but those who are asking insist on her foreignness. "German...?" they say "But you cannot be German." They point to her skin and recall its incompatibility with the national culture. This act of placing the Black subject outside the nation also warns us that we should 'know our place' instead of 'taking our place.' When Alicia says that she is Afro-German, she is 'taking her place' and at the same time reminding her audience that she, 'like the rest of them,' is 'at home' in 'her place.' But, her *white* surroundings react with nervousness, disquiet and aggression, promptly restaging a colonial order: "Oh! No, no! But you are not German (...) Where are you from?" Alicia's answer remains unheard: "They just start laughing, as if I misunderstood the question or gave the wrong answer." Indeed they fear to listen that Germany has, among others, an Afro-German history. The sound of contemptuous *white* laughter announce how the *white* subject is, de facto, invested in the fantasy that only *whites* can be German and that Germany is *white* – a fantasy that rules their reality.

> Racism is not only insulting, but first of all, how people look at you... when people come to ask: "Where are you from? Why do you speak German that good?" This is racism... and these forms of racism disturb me even more.

Alicia describes the *white* subject's look as disturbing, for it reflects a frighteningly deformed self-image that she cannot recognize as herself: "what do they see?" The disturbance provoked by the *white* gaze is derived not from something missing or something the *white* subject does not see in Alicia, but rather the addition of something undesirable that the *white* subject wants to see. In other words, racism is not a lack of information about the

'Other' – as it is commonly believed – but the *white* projection of undesirable information onto the 'Other.' Alicia can eternally explain that she is Afro-German, yet it is not her explanation that counts, but the deliberate addition of *white* fantasies of what she should be like: "Why do you speak German that good?"

Alicia may experience this contradiction as a painful inner splitting. On the one hand, she cannot recognize herself in the image they see; on the other hand, what they see separates Alicia from whatever identity she may really have. As she explains "these forms of racism disturb me even more."

3. "(...) THEY WANT TO HEAR AN EXOTIC STORY." – VOYEURISM AND THE JOY OF *OTHERNESS*

> And also the fact of not being seen as German, but as an exotic. Especially when men come and ask... I know they want to hear a very exotic story. They want to hear that I come from somewhere in Africa or Brazil, or... whatever.

Here, Alicia adds another component: 'race' and *voyeurism*. People come to ask where she is from because they also have pleasure through the exhibition of Otherness. They are not interested in hearing that Alicia is German just like them; rather "they want to hear a very exotic story," where their colonial fantasies about the remote 'Other' are revived.

Alicia is expected to provoke pleasure. Impatiently, question after question, her audience searches for 'paradise': "What about your parents, where are they from?" They keep asking until a fabulous exotic story is told. Exotic – Erotic. This is what has aptly been called *modern primitivism* (hooks 1992). Primitivism, in the sense that it constructs the Black subject as 'primitive,' as the one who is closer to nature, who possesses what *whites* have lost and what they are therefore excited by. Alicia then becomes the embodiment of exoticism and satisfaction. Sometimes this is called *positive racism*. But what a stupidity. Stupid indeed to call racism positive. This term this is a paradoxical one. It contradicts itself, as exclusion, isolation and racial exposure can never be positive.

> I do not have the story that I look like. I feel that I don't have any story at all, because my story – the German story, the Afro-German story – is not welcome. They don't want to hear it or to know it.

It seems one can only exist through as an alienated image of oneself. The moment the Black subject is inspected from the outside as a fetish object, an object of obsession and desire, is described by Frantz Fanon as a process of 'absolute depersonalization' (1967: 63), for one is forced to develop a relationship to the self and give a performance of the self that has been scripted by the colonizer, producing in oneself the internally divided condition of depersonalization. One starts looking at oneself *as if one were in their place*: "I feel that I don't have any story at all," Alicia concludes. She has started experiencing herself as 'Other' among the others – isolated in a *white* society.

CHAPTER 6

HAIR POLITICS

4. "(...) PEOPLE USED TO TOUCH MY HAIR!" – *INVADING* THE BLACK BODY

> What I really hated was that people used to touch my hair: "Such beautiful hair! Oh, what interesting hair! Look, Afro hair..." And they touch it. I felt like a dog that is being caressed... like a dog that is being touched. And I am not a dog, I'm a person. And [when I was a child] my mother never told them to stop that, although I explained her that I didn't like it. But she couldn't understand why I didn't like it: "Yes, but your hair is different and people are just curious!" She didn't understand why I didn't like it. (...) I would never touch somebody's hair, just like that. I mean... how can somebody do that...

Here, Alicia is told she is 'different.' But who is different? I ask again. Is Alicia different from those who touch her hair or, the way around, are those who touch her hair 'different from her? Who is different from whom? One only becomes different, in the moment one is told to differ from those who have the power to define themselves as 'normal.' Alicia's *white* mother does not see herself as different, but rather her daughter. That is, one is not different, one is made different through a process of discrimination.

Difference is used as a mark for intrusion. Being touched, just like being questioned, is experienced as an intrusion, an infringement that for Alicia seems unimaginable: "I would never touch somebody's hair." Why should she touch the hair of someone she does not know? Why such an intrusion? Those who touch and/or ask mark Alicia, they however remain unmarked. A choreography that describes whiteness as both central and absent.

Despite the ambiguous comments – which sometimes seem *positive* – the power relation between those who touch and Alicia, who is being touched, nevertheless remains, along with the disdainful role of becoming a public object. Alicia's mother however seems to confirm the situation rather than dispel it: "[When I was a child] my mother never told them to stop...," she explains "she didn't understand." Alicia sadly realizes that her *white* mother identifies not with her Black daughter, but with her *white* surroundings: "(...) your hair is different and people are just curious," explains the mother. The comment is a reminder to Alicia that even in this relationship, her standpoint as a Black woman is less valid than the standpoint of her *white* mother and the *white* consensus.[21] The 'Black woman' says it matters and

---

21 See *triangulation*, episodes: 8, 10, 17 and 25.

the '*white* woman' responds, 'it does not matter!' This division mirrors how neither can escape colonial relations – unfortunately. Alicia's mother seems unable to listen to her daughter's words; they speak not of her world, but of a world of racism and aggression.

'Not listening' is a strategy that protects the *white* subject from acknowledging the subjective world of Black people, as I will explore later. Historically, it has been used as a mark of oppression in that it negates Black people's subjectivity and personal accounts of racism.

> anyway... if I would insist she would often start crying: "what do you want me to do?" I would feel so terribly bad that I wouldn't dare to mention it again for a while. At the end I always had to comfort her... "it's ok!..."

Regression is deeply linked with this process, as the *white* subject often avoids or seek to avoid anxiety and guilt by returning to a previous stage of development. The infantile patterns of behaviour, such as being annoyed, irritated, offended or crying remain available as defense not to deal with the information. So, when the Black subject declares racism, like a child, the *white* subject reverts to an immature behaviour, becoming again the central character who needs attention, while the Black subject is placed as secondary. The dynamic between both is turned up-side-down, this is what in classic psychoanalysis is called regression.

5. "EXCUSE ME, HOW DO YOU WASH YOUR HAIR?" – FANTASIES OF DIRTINESS AND COLONIAL DOMESTICATION[22]

> And sometimes people come and ask questions like: "How do you wash your hair?" Or they want to know if I comb it: "Do you comb your hair? How do you do it?" I find this so sick and so sad, you know. Our hair looks different, but it does not cross my mind to see a *white* adult woman and ask her: "Excuse me, how do you wash your hair? And by the way, do you also comb it?" What a question. How do I wash my hair? Well, with water and shampoo, like everybody else. Sometimes I ask myself, what is it that they really want to say, when they ask these questions. I mean... *(laughs)* How does somebody dare

---

22 Parts of this episode were published in Kilomba 2003.

to ask such questions to a woman, to an adult Black woman, [whether] she washes herself? What's in their mind? I don't know... Well, I know, but I do not even want to think about it!

Alicia describes these questions as 'sick' and 'sad' because they reveal an association with Blackness that is nauseating; they announce how in the *white* imaginary Black women are in some way fantasized as dirty and wild. Both dirtiness and wildness are inscribed within each single question: "How do you wash your hair" because it is dirty and "do you comb it" because it looks wild. An insulting alignment of colonial thoughts: wash/dirt, comb/wild.

Dirtiness and wildness are closely linked with aspects of what *white* society has repressed – sexuality and aggression – and consequently projected onto 'Others.' Often sexuality is combined with aggression and experienced as 'dirty,' in which case thoughts will be 'doubly denied' (Pajaczkowska and Young 1992: 201). Alicia sees herself being used as a deposit for those doubly denied aspects, as she becomes the double embodiment of sexuality (dirt) and aggression (wildness). *White* people's concern with the hygiene of the Black woman reveals, on the one hand the *white* desire to control the Black body; on the other hand, the *white* fear of being dirtied by that body. "How do you wash yourself" and "how clean are you" are the translated questions. These indicate how the presence of the Black subject triggers both desire and fear. There is a 'fear of racial contagion' (Marriot 1998). The word contagion is quite evocative because it describes how in the *white* unconscious Blackness is fantasized as a disease, a 'corporeal malediction' (Fanon 1967: 112), that the *white* subject is afraid of being contaminated with.

With certain irony, Alicia states that it would not cross her mind to ask a *white* woman how she washes her hair or whether she combs it. The apparent irony resides in the fact that such questions are senseless to Alicia, as shown in the open-ended remark, "What a question. How do you wash your hair? Well, with water and shampoo, like everybody else." The questions are meaningless and somehow ridiculous, ironic and even absurd, making Alicia laugh. It is, however, a bitter laugh, for these ridiculous questions also embody the crueler irony of her imprisonment as the dirty 'Other.'

6. "(...) ME AND MY NATURAL HAIR." – HAIR, BLACK WOMEN AND POLITICAL CONSCIOUSNESS

> Once I had a (*white*) boyfriend – I used to have braids – and one day I opened the braids and just combed my hair, like this natural, Afro hair, very beautiful (*touching her hair*). And when he saw me, he started insulting me, saying: "Why did you do that, do you want to look ugly?... Look at you, look at your hair, you look like a sheep!" That was very hard for me... he could not accept me... he could not accept me with my natural hair. Even today it is like that, many Black women are concerned about their hair... they straighten their hair... Once a woman said to me, "Well, I would like so much to have falling hair, but my hair stands, just like Alicia's!" It was clear that she was saying that our hair is not good, that is what she is told everyday. Even Black top models like Naomi Campbell, she has to straighten her hair, you never saw how her real hair looks like. Isn't that crazy? You never saw her really African hair! It is hard... because when you have your hair natural people insult you. I was insulted on the street several times, like: "Do you know what a comb is?! Oh, welcome to the jungle! (*singing*) Why don't you do your hair?" I ask myself what is so disturbing about our hair?

Here, Alicia speaks of hair, political consciousness, and everyday racism and its internalization. She talks about a *white* boyfriend who one day insulted her for showing her natural hair. The words of her boyfriend divulge a combination of shame and repugnance toward Alicia, but above all they restage a colonial association.

Historically, Black people's unique hair was devalued as the most visible stigma of Blackness and used to justify the subordination of Africans (Banks 2000, Byrd and Tharps 2001, Mercer 1994). More than skin color, hair became the most potent mark of servitude during the enslavement period. Once Africans were enslaved, skin color was tolerated by *white* masters, but not hair, which became a symbol of 'primitivity,' disorder, inferiority and un-civilization. African hair was then classified as 'bad hair.' At the same time, Black people were pressured to relax 'bad hair' with the appropriate chemicals, developed by European industries. These were forms of controlling and erasing the so-called 'repulsive signs' of Blackness.

In this context, hair became the most important instrument of political consciousness among Africans and African Diasporic people. Dreadlocks, Rasta, Afro-hair and African hairstyles convey a political message of racial empowerment and a protest against racial oppression. They are politicized and shape Black women's positions concerning 'race,' gender and beauty. In other words, they reveal how we negotiate identity politics and racism – ask Angela Davis!

Alicia's hairstyle can thus be seen as a political statement of racial awareness in which she redefines dominant patterns of beauty. The insults, however, respond with disapproval to such redefinition and reveal *white* anxiety about losing control over the colonized. In a certain way, the insults warn Alicia that she is becoming *too* Black by showing *too* many signs of Blackness; they might also signify that she was showing signs of independence and decolonization toward *white* norms, a disturbing fact for her *white* public: "Why did you do that? Look at you, look at your hair," she is told. "He could not accept me with my natural hair."

Becoming *too* Black is at the same time associated with the idea of regressing to primitivity: "Do you know what a comb is?! Oh, welcome to the jungle!" as they sang to Alicia. There is thus a relation between racial awareness and decolonization of the Black body, as well as between racist insults and control of the Black body. In order to avoid such violent insults, says Alicia, many Black women see themselves forced to deracialize the most significant sign of racialization: "Black women straighten [their] hair... because when you have your hair natural, people insult you." But this process of having to fabricate signs of whiteness, such as relaxed hair, and to encounter *white* patterns of beauty in order to avoid public humiliation is rather violent. Also violent is this rapid metamorphosis from a person into an animal: "You look like a sheep!"

7. "HE SMELLED MY HAIR AND MADE THIS ASSOCIATION... WITH MONKEYS" – *WHITE* WILD FANTASIES, LOVE AND THE BLACK VENUS

> After washing my hair I usually put some coconut butter... coconut cream, it smells very good and the hair gets very smooth... and... I had a short relationship with a [*white*] man, a flirt... and one day, he was smelling my hair, and said: "Well, your hair smells of coconuts ..." And then he started singing this song: "*Die Affen rasen durch den Wald, der eine machte den anderen kalt. Wer hat die Kokosnuss geklaut?*"[23] Do you

---

23 *T.* "The monkeys run fast through the forest. One kills the other... Who has stolen the coconuts?"

know that German song? (*she sings*) "*Wer hat die Kokosnuss, wer hat die Kokosnuss, wer hat die Kokosnuss geklaut?*" And he sang this song, and I was so... so... and he said: "But your hair smells like coconut cream!" He smelled my hair and made this association... with monkeys, monkeys in the jungle who have stolen coconuts... you understand? He associated me with monkeys... and this song... I was so destroyed... I wasn't very long in this relation because I couldn't stand him anymore. But worse is that he was a very German intellectual, an archaeologist, who did his Ph.D. in Archaeology.

Alicia recalls a *white* boyfriend who smelled the fragrance of coconuts in her hair and started singing the German colonial song[24]: "*Die Affen rasen durch den Wald, der eine machte den anderen kalt. Wer hat die Kokosnuss geklaut?*" Alicia is upset by the association of smelling the fragrance of coconuts in a Black woman's hair and a song about 'barbaric' monkeys. The song recalls a long history of colonial discourse where Black people were metaphorically represented as monkeys. The metaphor of 'the African' as 'monkey' became effectively real, not because it is a biological fact, but because racism functions through discourse. Racism is not biological, but discursive. It functions through a discursive regime, a chain of words and images that by association become equivalents: African – Africa – jungle – wild – primitive – inferior – animal – monkey.[25]

---

24 Another component of this song, which I will not analyze here, is the *white* desire to eliminate the Black subject. This is a typical theme in European colonial songs, where Black subjects kill each other in the jungle or die one after the other due to their incapacity to survive as independent subjects, such as in "10 kleiner *N*.," originally called "10 *N*.," a song composed during the abolishment of slavery in the USA and later translated into German to coincide with the loss of the German colonial empire. There is a clear association between the idea of Black independence and plague; that is, once the Black subject is free, her/his presence is overwhelming and intolerable.

25 Illustrative examples of these associative chains of words and images are films produced during the most critical period of the European colonial project, such as "Tarzan" or "King Kong," where the *white* hero has as counterpart an African monkey. Tarzan and Jane share their lives with Chiquita, a female monkey, while in "King Kong," the female protagonist is seduced by a gigantic male gorilla. The viewer is invited to look at Africa (the setting) as a place of monkeys (Africans) and *white* heros (colonizers). Still, in the most recent Walt Disney productions, Africa is the only continent whose story is (re)presented by animals instead of people and their cultures, as in "The Lion King." All other continents and cultures are represented by people such as "Pocahontas" (portraying a Native American legend) or "Mulan" (portraying a Chinese legend), among others.

Such chains of association become convincing because they signify through a process of *displacement*. The psychoanalytical notion of displacement refers to the process by which the individual transfers interest from one mental image to another, detaching attention from the first and passing it to a second that is related to the initial by way of association. Displacement, for instance, is responsible for how in dreams one image becomes the symbol of another. Displacement also has a defensive function, particularly within phobia and censorship. The individual shifts interest from one object to another in such a way that the latter becomes either an equivalent or substitute for the first. This process in which the latter object, 'the monkey,' becomes a symbol of the former, 'the African,' allows censored discourses – racist discourses – to take place without necessarily being perceived as aggressive; after all, this is a song about monkeys and coconuts. Such associative chains transform the Black woman – Black Venus – savage Black – human savage – savage animal – animal.

The same associative chains are also visible in the debate on national identity discussed in the first episode, where *national 'Others'* are often defined as *Ausländer* or immigrants, and immigrants are often defined as *illegal immigrants*. If immigrants are *illegal*, they are *lawless*; if they are lawless, they are *criminals*; if they are criminals, they are *dangerous*; if they are dangerous, one *fears* them; if one fears them, one has the right to be hostile or even to eliminate them. A chain of equivalents legitimates racism by fixing identities in their place: immigrants – illegal immigrants – lawless – criminal – dangerous – fearful.

Alicia does demonstrate her shock, but the boyfriend does not take responsibility for what he has said. He, as a *white* man, dissociates himself from what he sings to the Black woman, creating a neutral arena. In psychoanalytical terms *dissociation* reveals exactly this state where two or more mental processes co-exist without becoming connected or integrated: "But your hair does smell like coconuts!" he responds to Alicia. Such dissociation depoliticizes the song, saving the *white* boyfriend from having to develop any consciousness of himself as responsible.

The song depicts *white* representations of colonized territories and their people: animals living in chaos, disorder and un-civilization, with the jungle as setting. These were forms of propaganda used to justify the European project of colonial occupation, in order to domesticate and civilize the 'Other.' The song, just like images, can be analyzed in three different stages: first its lyrics: "There are monkeys in Africa, fighting over a coconut"; then its message: "Africans can also fight over a coconut, just like monkeys." Its code, however, is: "Africans are meant to be monkeys." While the lyrics present the characters of a scene, the message introduces the problematic in this scene. It is the code, however, that is registered in our unconscious, introducing 'Africans' as 'monkeys.'

The boyfriend delivers both the code and message of the song, but insists that he is only singing the lyrics. Violent associations of Blackness with primitiveness, chaos, disorder and conquest are being performed and negated at the same time. This abusive situation reminds Alicia of the alienating – or, as she says, schizophrenic – condition of experiencing racism:

(...) Sometimes, I have to ignore... not ignore, I have to *verdrängen* [*T.* repress], pretend I forgot everything. It is as if I have to cut it from myself, to cut my personality like a schizophrenic. As if some parts of me didn't exist.

CHAPTER 7

SEXUAL POLITICS

8. "WER HAT ANGST VOR DEM SCHWARZEM MANN"[26] – THE OEDIPUS COMPLEX, KILLING THE BLACK MAN AND SEDUCING THE BLACK WOMAN

I remember once, me and my ex-boyfriend (a young *white* man) were in a café together... we used to go to cafés and have long, long conversations about nothing... nothing special. We used to spend a long time there. He was a jazz musician, and I remember one day he was telling me what kind of jokes he and his musician friends used to tell. And I remember asking him to tell me... I mean, they were all going to be sexist little jokes, I thought, the kind of jokes men tell. I don't even remember what they were, but nothing really terrible... And then he said: "Well, I know one joke, but I can't really tell you..." And I said: "Oh, come on, tell me, tell me, tell me..." And he didn't want to, I admit he didn't want to tell me. But then he finally did. He got a piece of paper and design... you got a piece of paper? (*she asks me*)... and he drew this... (*Kathleen draws a circle with two triangles inside*). And then he asked me: "What is it about?" And I looked and I said: "It looks like a Red Cross sign that has been erased..." And I didn't know what this was, and he said: "There's two Ku Klux Klan members looking down at the Black man, who was thrown into a (dark) hole!" And this was a joke... a joke that he told me... And I had that feeling again, that ache in my hands... Oh! That came over me so fast... And he saw it, and he said: "I'm sorry, I'm sorry." I mean, he apologized immediately. And it was this feeling of... somebody that you have been sharing intimate things with and suddenly this comes out...

These are the words of Kathleen, an African-American woman living in Germany. Kathleen describes everyday racism within an intimate relationship, as her boyfriend tells her a joke about an historical reality in which Black people, and Black men in particular, were systematically beaten, lynched

---

26 T. *Who's afraid of the Black man?* is a game played by very young children (between the ages of 2 and 10) in kindergarten and at school in Germany. One plays the role of the Black man and asks the other children if they are afraid of him – "Wer hat Angst vor dem Schwarzen Mann?" – to which they answer, screaming, "Keine!" (T. *No one!*) and run away in alarm, while the 'Black man' runs after them, saying: "Und wenn er kommt dann lauf ihr!" (T. *So when he comes, run away!*) The children run in panic, trying to escape from the 'Black man,' who is now chasing them. Despite many protests, this game is still played in many kindergartens and schools in Germany.

and even killed by members of the Ku Klux Klan (KKK) in the US. [27] In the joke, a Black man is thrown into a hole by two members of the KKK. The image of the 'hole' is quite illustrative because it describes a hierarchy between the space above and the space below. The Black man is thrown into the 'hole' and placed below the feet of the *white* men.

It seems the boyfriend has certain amusement in this racial subjugation, as he speaks about the violence against the Black man and incurs pain in the Black woman, Kathleen, in the form of a hilarious joke. As Kathleen is sadistically being told a joke about Black subjugation, she is also symbolically thrown into this same 'hole,' below the feet of the *white* boyfriend. This combination of violence and amusement characterizes racial sadism. He enjoys the subjugation of both the Black man and the Black woman: "Well, I know a joke, but I can't really tell you..." he says to Kathleen. "Tell me, tell me..." she replies – expecting to hear something else. Racist jokes have the sadistic function of getting pleasure from inflicting pain and humiliation on the racial 'Other,' giving her/him a sense of loss toward the *white* subject. Kathleen loses the sense of predictability and safety. This loss, on the other hand, secures *white* supremacy. While Kathleen feels in danger, her boyfriend feels certain amusement, even if just for a short moment; like in the joke itself, where the *white* men above enjoy looking down at the endangered Black man. The joke is more than a narration; it becomes an experience in itself. It is a simultaneous game in which the script is synchronically performed both inside and outside, as Kathleen experiences the pain of the Black character in the joke: "I had that feeling again, that ache in my hands," she says. "Oh! That came over me so fast..."

Racist jokes reinforce *white* superiority and the idea that Black people should remain in subordinate positions – in the 'hole.' They express *white*

---

27 The Ku Klux Klan was organized in Tennessee (USA) in 1865 by a group of Confederate army officers who adapted their name from the Greek word *Kuklos* ("circle"). The Ku Klux Klan began as a fraternal organization, and was soon directed against Republican Reconstruction, whose main political platform was the abolition of slavery and civil equality for former slaves. In the 1920s the Klan expanded rapidly and was particularly active in the 1960s. The Klan used violence and intimidation against both public officials and Black people in general to prevent them from voting, holding office and exercising their new rights. Many freewomen and freemen, as well as *white*s who supported Reconstruction, were kidnapped, flogged, lynched, mutilated and murdered by the Ku Klux Klan. Between 1882 and 1935, more than 3,000 Black people were lynched in public, and between 1882 and 1955, over 4,700 Black people died in mob action. The Ku Klux Klan is still active in the United States and Canada (www.africana.com).

reluctance to renounce racist ideology. That is why Kathleen is shocked listening to the joke: she is being introduced to another side of her boyfriend. Such jokes, writes Philomena Essed, permits the expression of racist feelings by "expecting or hoping for consent from others by way of laughter" (1991: 257). Those supposedly funny comments, racist jokes and forms of ridicule are integrated in casual conversation and presented as casual comments in order to ventilate their real racist meanings. Power and hostility against Blacks are exercised without being necessarily criticized or even identified – a joke is only a joke.

The whole episode takes place in two different arenas: a physical one with the boyfriend and Kathleen, and a phantasmal one with the boyfriend and his *white* musician friends. In both, Kathleen is singled out in a triangular constellation, physically surrounded by the boyfriend and the *white* audience seated in the café, and phantasmally surrounded by the boyfriend and his *white* musician friends. "[T]elling (*Kathleen*) what kind of jokes he and his musician friends used to tell," the boyfriend creates a triangle, making sure he is not alone before he performs racism. The existence of this third element – the *white* public – reinforces not only Kathleen's isolation, but also the power position of the young man, who is surrounded by 'his own group.' Such a triangular constellation permits the *white* subject to perform racism against the Black subject without being publicly judged because he knows that his group – the so-called *white* consensus – will certainly support him. They support him as they support themselves. Because of its repressive function, the triangular constellation of Black people as solo and *whites* as a collective allows everyday racism to be performed. I wonder if the boyfriend would have told this joke had he been in a Black setting, in a café surrounded by Black people, or had Kathleen brought some Black friends. He would have been in serious trouble!

The entire scene involves a certain seduction, inasmuch as the aggressor takes the initiative of offering something to which Kathleen submits passively. The scene of seduction is experienced passively, first, because Kathleen is involved in a passive way during the entire scene; she listens to him, looks at his drawing, is asked and answers his questions, and second, because she participates in the seduction, 'tolerating' it without being able to evoke a response. This state of passivity and unpredictability implies an absence of preparation, as Kathleen was expecting "nothing really terrible" – she was not anticipating racism. Apparently, the young man transfers responsibility for his racist action to the 'victim,' as if he has been acting on Kathleen's request. She becomes guilty, as she repeatedly says: "I admit he didn't want to tell (…) he didn't want to," but she asked him to. Because racism is not seen as a societal phenomenon, those who face racism are always confronted with the message that their experiences are due to their own personal over-sensitivity and their own responsibility. In this way, the boyfriend does not feel responsible for seducing Kathleen with a racist joke, but rather Kathleen herself. She overtakes his responsibility, as victims of aggression usually do, protecting their aggressors by taking over their feelings of shame and guilt.

> I realized how much of myself I have out at risk (…) I don't know why he was with me or why I was with him, that's also a question… (*laughs*). I was naive. And why was he with me, I don't know… He was a pianist and he was obsessed with jazz. A very good pianist, technically very talented. I wouldn't say that he wanted to be Black… maybe (…) (*silence*) I do think that *white* men in this country are very attracted to Black women. I think that there is something exciting about Black women that they definitely want to have.

The joke in which two *white* men beat a Black man is deeply connected with both desire and envy. The boyfriend, a *white* jazz musician, is symbolically murdering the Black man in front of Kathleen. On the one hand, he plays the music of the Black man, desiring him; on the other hand, he enjoys joking about the Black man being thrown into a 'hole' by two *white* men – envy and the destruction of the envied object.

The lynching of Black men – where repressed sexuality and physical possession are so closely interwoven that they merge – is the cruelest example of this racial envy. Historical archives reveal how until the 1950s Black men lynched in the southern US were nearly always subjected to rituals of castration. The simultaneous murder of the Black male and the possession of the Black penis mirror the connection between desire, envy and destruction. Lynching was a powerful form of humiliating Black men and discrediting their patriarchal status and their masculinity in a society ruled by *white* males. When the boyfriend tells the joke, he is also castrating Black men by presenting them as subjugated, humiliated males.

It is worth linking the idea of the triangle of racism to the psychoanalytical concept of the Oedipus complex, as we are dealing with *white* hostile wishes toward the Black subject. This desire for the death of the rival – the Black man – and the sexual desire for the Black woman are extraordinarily visible in this episode. The jealous hatred for the Black man is such that he is killed by the boyfriend and the two *white* KKK members. In fact, the conflict is based on a triangular relationship. The aggression toward the racial 'Other' satisfies the *white* subject's destructive drive toward her/his own parents. The *white* subject apparently satisfies her/his repressed hatred for the mother/father only through the real and symbolic murder of the Black woman/man. This allows positive feelings for the family to remain intact while ambivalent emotional ties to the mother/father are allowed to appear – as an unconscious fantasy of racial intrusion – through substitute objects. "*Wer hat Angst vor dem Schwarzen Mann? – Keine!*" In other words, the Black subject becomes the element of hatred, substituting the real rivals. In this case, the boyfriend cannot kill his father – the rival – instead he 'kills' the Black man, who becomes his object of hate and seduces the Black woman, who like his mother is the object of desire. Within the triangle of racism the *white* subject attacks or kills the Black subject to make room for her/himself since she/he cannot attack or kill her/his own parent – at least not without being penalized. For this reason Frantz Fanon (1967) claims that the Oedipus complex is virtually a Western phenomenon. A colonized Black family does not mirror the colonizing nation; the Oedipus struggle does not allow the Black child to gain power in a colonial society commanded by *white* subjects. There is disharmony between childhood socialization and the expectations of adulthood, and as a result of this, Fanon argues, the conflict arises not from within the kinship group, but from contact with the *white* outside world.

9. "(...) AS IF WE ARE GOING TO TAKE THEIR MEN OR THEIR CHILDREN" – FANTASIES OF THE BLACK WHORE vs. BLACK MAMMY

When I see *white* mothers with Black children, I see they fear me and... There's this image of the Black woman who's going to steal their children, and with men it's different, they don't really fear us, it's more a sexual thing... [*white*] women see us as [competition], as if we are going to take their men or their children. When I sometimes walk on the street, and there's a couple, for example, and if I look at the man or at the woman, I can feel that they feel strange... I have this impression. Or a *white* woman with a child, especially when it is a Black child, she doesn't want that you look at her child.

This fantasy of Black women stealing children and men is very much in congruence with colonial memories. Historically Black women have had the function of both sexualized bodies and the breeders of workers (Collins 2000; hooks 1981, 1992); that is, the function of both lovers and mothers.

During slavery, Black women were sexually exploited to breed children. In her essay *Sexism and the Black Female Slave Experience*, bell hooks (1981) writes about how in advertisements announcing the sale of slaves, African women were described by their capacity to breed. They were classified as 'breeding slaves,' 'child-bearing women,' within the 'breeding period,' or 'too old to breed' (hooks 1981: 39). These were the categories used to describe individual Black women. During colonialism, their labor was used to nourish and provide for the *white* household while their bodies were used as nursing bottles where *white* children suckled milk. These are very imponent images of Blackness and motherhood.

The fear that Black women might steal children, as described by Alicia, can be linked to the unconscious image of Black women as *ideal* mothers. I recall that Roma and Sinti have a similar function in the *white* imaginary: 'Roma,' it is commonly said, 'are dangerous because they come to steal children.' There is a strong link between Otherness and the search for affection and motherhood. When Alicia talks about how *white* mothers do not want her, a Black woman, to look at their children, she seems to describe this fear. And since some of the *white* women Alicia describes have Black children, Alicia is not only imagined to be the ideal mother, but the *real* mother of their Black children.

This image of the Black woman as a 'mammy' has been serving as a social control of 'race,' gender and sexuality. It is a controlling image which confines Black women to the function of the maternal servant, justifying their subordination and economic exploitation. The 'mammy' represents the ideal Black female relationship to whiteness: as loving, nurturing, reliable, obidient and devoted servant, who is loved by the white family.

However, Alicia refers not only to this fear of the 'Black mother,' but to the *white* female fear of the 'sexualized Black woman' and *white* male desire. If *white* women seem to fear Alicia stealing their men, *white* men in turn see her as a desirable sexualized body. These images of Black womanhood are 'a reservoir' for the fears of western culture, where the Black 'mammy' and the 'sexually aggressive Black whore' come to represent those female functions that a 'puritan society' cannot confront: the body, fertility and sexuality. Racism therefore constructs Black womanhood as double – the 'asexual obedient servant' and the 'sexualized primitive whore' (Hall 1992). It is a doubling process whereby fear and desire for the Other double for one another.

Like in the last episode, in this heterosexual constellation there is a triangulation. Also here we can link both seduction and hostility towards Alicia with the Oedipus complex, as the rival of the *white* woman is the Black woman, while the Black man is her object of desire – from whom she has a child – and vice versa, the *white* male sexualizes the Black woman, but killed the Black man previously.

10. "I WAS [COMPETITION] FOR HER BECAUSE I WAS BLACK LIKE HER CHILD" – BLACK WOMEN, BLACK CHILDREN, *WHITE* MOTHERS

And once I was [on the street] distributing little postcards of an Afro-shop from a friend of mine, and gave it mostly to Black people, and there was this *white* mother with a Black child passing and, of course, I gave it to her... and she refused. She walked away, pushing the child. It was a strange situation, it felt like... she saw a Black woman coming in her direction, giving her something and she could not deal with it... she was not curious or so, no... She was afraid, kind of irritated, as if she didn't want to have nothing to do with Black matters, but it happens that she has a Black child! I was very angry with this woman... very upset, she reminded me of my mother, this kind of attitude. She refused because Black children are very cute, they are like chocolate... but the adults are something threatening. I was threatening for her, and I also was [competition] for her because I was Black like her child, and she was *white*.

Alicia describes a triangle that reminds her of the relationship between her, her mother and the Black people they sometimes encountered on the street. An uncomfortable triangle in which the Black woman identifies with the Black child; the Black child is pushed aside by the *white* mother; and the *white* mother refuses contact with the Black woman.

This description reminds us how such a triangulation is dominated by the ambivalence of whiteness. The mother seems to have two co-existing views: one that perceives the Black child as 'good,' 'cute,' 'like chocolate,' and another that experiences the Black adult woman as fearsome, irritating and troubling, someone the mother wants to avoid. The whole passage describes the anxiety of an encounter marked by competition rather than identification. Who can identify with whom? The Black child with the Black woman? Or with the *white* woman, her own mother? The Black woman with the Black child, who reminds her of herself? The Black woman with the *white* woman, who reminds her of her own mother and of herself as a future mother? Or does the *white* woman identify with the Black woman, who reminds her of her daughter, a woman-to-be?

Such identifications are shuttered by racism, for the child is pushed away from Alicia, causing an irreparable separation between them. This separation raises a primary and conflictive question for the Black child: To whom should she be loyal? To her *white* mother or the Black woman?

CHAPTER 8

SKIN POLITICS

11. "WELL, BUT *FOR ME* YOU ARE NOT BLACK!" – RACIAL PHOBIA AND RECOMPENSE

> Once this woman – we were together at school and we were still friends after school – and once we had this conversation about Black people and I told her how it is being Black here [in Germany] and that it is not easy for me always to be the only Black person, and she said: "Well, but for me you are not Black! I don't think that you are Black! I even forget that you are Black!"... er... and she said that in a way, as if she was doing me a favor. But I AM BLACK! That is what my adoptive mother did all the time, she denied that we were Black children, me and my brother. She said nothing, she never said a word... we never talked about it when I was little.

This passage shows the process of invisibilizing the visible. When Alicia reveals to her *white* friend her own reality as a Black woman, the friend suddenly responds by saying that she is not Black. What was seen becomes suddenly unseen. Alicia is unexpectedly fantasized as colorless. This sudden inability to *see* 'race' once it is mentioned by those who are marked as racialized seems related to a massive mechanism of negation[28] where Blackness is only admitted to consciousness in its negative form: "I <u>don't</u> think that you are Black! I even forget that you are Black!" This is disturbing to Alicia. When she reveals her disquieting reality as a Black woman, she is at the same time being told that her Blackness is not significant.

Such ambivalent confessions prevent *whites* in everyday life from being confronted with Black people's reality and the ways in which we perceive, experience and feel this reality (Essed 1991). Moreover, it prevents the *white* subject from having to deal with the uncomfortable fact that there are differences and that these differences occur through processes of discrimination. At this moment of revelation, the Black subject is suddenly told to be colorless: "Well, but for me you are not Black!" The interruption within the sentence "but <u>for me</u> you are not" reminds Alicia not only of *white* fears and anxieties about Blackness, but also of how her own life has been shaped by

---

28 In German, '*Verneinung*' denotes *negation* in the logical and grammatical sense, but it also means *denial* in the psychological sense of rejection of a statement I have made or that has been imputed to me, e.g. 'No, I did not say that, I did not think that.' In this second sense, *Verneinung* comes close to *Verleugnung*: to disown, deny, disavow, or refute (Laplanche and Pontalis 1988: 262).

the fear of being attacked by phobic intrusions (Marriott 1998). The phobia in this scenario resides in the mechanism of negation, which convey how one is hated from without: "You are not Black." What would happen if those who negate seeing her Blackness were to suddenly see it? And why can they not see it in the first place? Why do they need to negate it? Alicia realizes how Black people are fantasized as negative in the *white* collective unconscious and notes how her friend rushes to reject such a fantasy: "She even said that (...) as if she was doing me a favor" – the 'favor' of not identifying Alicia with the negative.

"But I AM BLACK!" she says, affronted. Within this racial phobia, Black people only become Black when they are considered the intruding 'Other,' the so-called *wild fremd*,[29] but since Alicia is seen by her friend as neither *wild* nor *fremd* by her friend, she is instantly not Black at all: "[No], but for me you are not Black." This allows positive feelings for Alicia to remain intact while repugnant and aggressive feelings toward Blackness are projected onto the outside. Here we can understand the function of '*political correctness*,' it protects us from the toxic imaginary of the *white* subject. Our concern is not what the *white* subject thinks, but rather the fact that we do not want to be invaded by its toxic and dirty fantasies.

12. "MY ADOPTIVE PARENTS USED THE WORD 'N.' ALL THE TIME. FOR ME THEY USED THE WORD 'M.'..." – RACISM WITHIN THE FAMILY

My adoptive parents always said *Neger*... they used the word *Neger* all the time. Even I was using it as a child, because I didn't know... and I grew up with this word. For me they used the word *Mischling*, which I didn't like, it was somehow strange... I knew something was wrong with this word, but it was different from *Neger*, somehow the word seemed less worse. The word *Neger* is very strong, very insulting... it hurts very much... *Mischling* too, but somehow it seemed less aggressive. So they saw me as a *Mischling*, not as a *Neger*.

---

29 The German expression '*wild fremd*,' correctly translated as 'wild stranger' or 'savage stranger,' is derived from the colonial period and nowadays is commonly used in everyday language to refer to a person one does not know. For instance, "*sie ist mir wild fremd*" – she is 'savagely' strange to me – means "I do not know her."

Categories such as the *N*-word and the *M*-word proclaim a racial hierarchy.[30] In describing how these categories were used by her family to define Black people, Alicia reveals the vulnerability of her position within her household.

These hostile colonial classifications remind Alicia that she occupies a kind of sub-category separating her from the '*N.*' as well as from *whites*; that is, she is neither among the rejected, nor among the accepted. As '*M.*' she is in between. Being called '*M.*' at the same time reveals an unmistakable hierarchy between light-skinned and dark-skinned Blacks, a hierarchy, to use Alicia's words, between the 'less worse' and the 'worse' description: "(F)or me they used the word '*M.*', which I didn't like (...) but it was different from '*N.*', somehow (...) less insulting." A strange word, she argues, a word anchored in European colonial history and revived during National Socialism in Germany. Even though the *M*-word was commonly used, she knew as a child that something was wrong with it.

The term '*M.*' was invented in the 17th century during the European expansion and is derived from the Latin *miscere*, meaning 'mixing,' or in German, 'mischen' or 'vermischen.' The verb 'mischen' combined with the suffix '-ling' make direct reference to a person. Symbolically, the term '*M.*' relates to the idea that one is '50/50' (*halb und halb*), 'mixed' (*gemischt*) or 'neither nor the other' (*weder das eine noch das andere*) marking those of mixed relationships as abnormal (Arndt & Hornscheidt 2004). However, it is the principle of racial superiority first and foremost – '*reine Rasse*' or '*Reinhaltung des Blutes*' – that gives the *M*-word its meaning. A child from a *white* 'mixed' French-German relationship, for example, is not categorized as '*M.*' – only a child whose parents are *white* and 'non-*white.*' This corresponds to an historical period during which relationships among Blacks and *whites* and their children were prohibited so as not to dirty the *white* 'race' with their offspring. During the Nazi era in Germany the *M*-word was largely used to label the children of forbidden unions between two 'races,' as they were seen as symbols of the degradation of the *aryan* 'race.'

In this sense, the term '*M.*' emerged as a sign of disturbance and inferiority, placing *white*ness as the absolute norm. That the term is synonymous with

---

30 Classification itself acts as a conceptual tool of colonialism. Its guiding principles are division and hierarchical ranking and its goal is mastery of the unknown. It is not accidental that scientists given the task of classifying plants, animals and humans often accompanied colonial ventures in 'opening' new territory for European economic and political use.

disturbance and inferiority is made clear in dictionaries, where the *M*-word is associated with other devaluating terms such as 'bastard,' analogous to 'illegitimate.' Meanwhile *Mulata* (fem.) or *Mulato* (masc.), both derived from the Portuguese *mula*, meaning 'mule' – the cross between a horse and a donkey – are specifically used to identify people of Black and *white* parentage; *Mestizo* (sp.), *métis* (fr.) or *mestiço* (port.) – meaning 'mongrel dog,' the cross between two dogs of two different 'races' – are terms used for people of Black or 'Indio' and *white* parentage. All of these terms have an offensive animal connotation and are related to the idea of infertility and prohibition. But, as Alicia recalls, "It seemed somehow less worse [than the *N*-word]. The *N*-word is very strong, very insulting... it hurts very much... '*M*.' too, but somehow it seemed less aggressive."

> And I always thought that I am not seen as a *Neger*, only Africans or very dark Black people were the *Negers*, but not me. And, of course, as a child I didn't want to have anything to do with them or to be like them, because every time I heard *white* people speaking about the *Neger* I realized it must be something threatening, something very... something that I absolutely don't want to have nothing to do with... Terrible, isn't it? Very terrible... very sad...

An alienating situation for Alicia, who is being taught by her *white* parents to fear who she is, Black; to fear other Black people, who then become '*N*.'s; and at the same to identify with what she will never be: *white*. I will explore this process of alienation in this passage while the origin of the *N*-word, its meaning and its traumatic significance will be explored in further episodes related by Kathleen.

"I always thought that I am not seen as a '*N*.'," Alicia says, "only Africans or very dark Black people (...) but not me." Her words make us aware of how she has been forced to identify with images of Blackness that are not desired, but imposed. The perception of oneself therefore occurs on the level of the *white* imaginary and is reinforced every day for the Black subject through colonial images, terminologies and languages. "It is in *white* terms that one perceives one's fellows," writes Fanon. "(P)eople will say of someone, for instance, that he is 'very black'; there is nothing surprising, within a family, in hearing a mother remark 'X is the blackest of my children' – it means that X is the least *white*" (1967: 163). Fanon's preoccupation is the fact that the Black subject can only exist in relation to the *white* other. One is forced to look at oneself *as if one were in their place*. Alicia indeed describes this process

95

when she recalls how in her childhood she wanted nothing to do with other Black people and wanted to be nothing like them because every time she heard *white* people speaking about the '*N*.', she realized it must be something very threatening. She was seeing herself as if she were *in their place*.

Yet, what else could she feel if the purpose of the *N*-word is exactly this, to describe the Black subject with both disgust and fear? An entire history of colonial oppression and racial stereotypes is reasserted in this term. "Terrible isn't it? Very terrible... very sad," concludes Alicia, recognizing how she has been taken over by a repulsive racial imago that really concerns not her, but the *white* imaginary.

13. "I DIDN'T WANT TO BE SEEN AS A 'N.,' LIKE THEY WERE" – MISREPRESENTATION AND IDENTIFICATION

[As a child] when Black people looked at me, I knew that I had something to do with them, but I didn't want to because I didn't want to be seen as a *Neger*, like they were. I thought there was something very wrong about it. There were all these very bad images of Black people in books, for example... or on the television, on the news, in the newspapers, basically everywhere. Everywhere... Still today, it is so... So, as a child I didn't want to be like them and at the same time I was one of them, and I knew it. A difficult situation...

This scenario – in which Alicia is now a child with a *white* mother, being looked at by other Black people – is the inverse of a previous passage in which she as an adult looks at other Black children. Here, she is not looking, but is instead being looked at. This gaze in particular, that of a Black adult looking at a Black child, was a disturbing experience for Alicia, not because of the dominance or control that the *white* gaze embodies, but because of the distress of the moment of identification. With whom can she identify? And what is she being identified with?

Even as she is being looked at, Alicia identifies the looker, but she cannot identify herself with what the looker comes to represent. *Identification* has two different dimensions: a *transitive* dimension in the sense that one 'identifies someone else,' and a *reflexive* one, in the sense of 'identifying with someone' (Laplanche & Pontalis 1988: 205-6). As a child, Alicia identified those who looked at her as people of the African Diaspora (transitive) and she knew she was one of them, but she could not identify with what they had come to symbolize both within and outside the family, the threatening '*N.*' (reflexive). This scene depicts the struggle the Black subject is made to submit to, a struggle to identify with *what one is,* but not with *how one is seen* in the *white* conceptual world.

Alicia was afraid to look at other Black people, not because of *what they were* – Black – but because of what Blackness *was seen as* – a threat. The fear of gazing back was in response to the overwhelming situation of having to identify with a threatening imago that she could not recognize as herself. This is not a struggle between a Black adult who is looking and a Black child who avoids looking back, but between the Black child and the *white* fantasies she has introjected. Quite a 'difficult situation' for the small Alicia: Who can she look at? And with whom can she identify? With the Black looker, who is identified as threatening? Or with the *white* mother, who identifies Blackness as a threat? The gaze of the Black subject becomes indeed disturbing because it exposes this very alienating reality. Maybe this conflict would not have taken place had her *white* mother, as Alicia says in previous episodes, reflected upon her own whiteness and been able to deal with Blackness. The child Alicia thus transports the conflict of her adult mother.

Another aspect raised in this passage is how the Black subject finds her/himself forced to identify with *white*ness because the images of Black people are not positive. "There were all these very bad images of Black people in books (...) or on television, on the news, in the newspapers, basically everywhere. Everywhere..." Alicia depicts the power of colonialism in the contemporary world. Even before a Black child has laid eyes on a *white* person, she/he has been bombarded with the message that *white*ness is both normative and superior, says Fanon. Magazines, comic books, films and television force the Black child to identify with *white* others, but not with her/himself. The child is forced to create an alienating relationship to Blackness, as the heroes of those scenarios are *white* and the Black characters are an embodiment of *white* fantasies. Only positive images, and I mean 'positive' not 'idealized' images, of Blackness created by Blacks themselves, in literature and visual culture, can dismantle this alienation, when one can finally identify positively with oneself and develop a positive self-image.

CHAPTER 9

THE N-WORD AND TRAUMA

14. "WHAT A BEAUTIFUL 'N.'!" – THE N-WORD AND TRAUMA[31]

I don't remember the first time that somebody actually physically put their hands on me, to check what Blacks feel like... it happens often that *white* people touch our hair or our skin to see what it feels like. I don't remember the very first time (...) But I remember my boyfriend had a piano teacher and I went after his piano lessons to pick him up. The piano teacher had a little girl, and the girl started talking about: "*Die schöne Negerin! Wie toll die Negerin aussieht. Die schönen Augen, die die Negerin hat! Und die schöne Haut, die die Negerin hat! Ich will auch Negerin sein!*" [*T.* The beautiful '*Negerin*'! Look how nice the '*Negerin*' looks. And the beautiful eyes that the '*Negerin*' has! And the beautiful skin that the '*Negerin*' has! I want to be a '*Negerin*' too!] And I heard this word: *N., N., N,. N.*, again and again.

An interesting combination of words, in which a positive word, 'beautiful,' is followed by a very traumatic one, the *N*-word. It is a game of sweet and bitter words that makes it difficult to identify racism. Kathleen is being called both: 'beautiful' and '*N*.' The first masquerades the second; the second, however, asserts her position as subordinate in relation to *white*s.

The *N*-word is not a neutral word, but a colonial concept invented during the European Expansion[32] to designate all sub-Saharan Africans (Essed 1991, Kennedy 2002). It is therefore a term placed within the history of slavery and colonization, linked to a collective experience of racial oppression, brutality and pain. In this episode I want to explore the direct relation between the spelling of the *N*-word and trauma – as Kathleen describes, the agonizing sound of the *N*-word "again and again."

Originally, the *N*-word was derived from the Latin word for the color black, *niger*. By the end of the 18th century, however, the *N*-word had already become a pejorative term, used strategically as a form of insult to implement feelings of loss, inferiority and submission before *white*s (Kennedy 2002).

---

31 Parts of this episode were published in Kilomba (2004).

32 I use the term 'European Expansion' to avoid the common colonial term 'discovery.' The idea of 'the discovery of Africa' can only exist when the continent is fantasized and conceptualized as a space with no previous history, a space whose history starts after the arrival of Europeans. The history, cultures and civilizations of African people therefore come to coincide with whiteness – a racist conception which is continuously reproduced in school as well as travellers book: "Angola: Angola was discovered by....," "Kenya: with the arrival of the..."

In this sense, when the *N*-word is spoken, one is referring not only to the (skin) color *black*, but also to a chain of terms that became associated with the word itself: primitivity – animality – ignorance – laziness – dirt – chaos, etc. This chain of equivalences defines racism. We become the embodiment of each one of these terms, not because they are physically inscribed on the surface of our skin and not because they are real, but because racism, as I mentioned earlier, is discursive rather than biological; it functions through discourse, through a chain of words and images that become associatively equivalent, holding identities in their place. Thus, being called '*N*.' is never simply being called *Black*; it is all the other analogies that define the function of the *N*-word.

This is experienced as a shock, depriving one of one's link to society. This violent shock is the first element of trauma. Upon hearing the *N*-word, Kathleen's link to society is abruptly broken, as she is being reminded that unconsciously this society is thought of as *white*. And in the eyes of the girl, Kathleen is merely a '*N*.'

The moment Kathleen is called '*N*.,' she is suddenly placed within a colonial scene. The term restages a relationship between *whites* and Blacks that is rooted in a master-slave dichotomy; those who call her '*N*.' recreate a scenario that reassures their power position as 'masters' and indicates the place Kathleen should occupy: the place of a '*N*.' "Look how nice the *N*. looks," the girl says about Kathleen. This moment of surprise and pain describes everyday racism as a mise-en-scéne, where *whites* suddenly become symbolic masters and Blacks, through insult and humiliation, become figurative slaves.

There is a *shame-pride* dynamic in this colonial relationship. While the Black woman is humiliated and dishonored in public, those who have insulted her have the chance to develop a sense of power and authority derived directly from her degradation. The scene thus revives a colonial trauma, the Black woman remains the vulnerable and exposed subject, and the *white* girl, although very young, remains the contented authority. The subordinate position of one (dishonor/shame) guarantees the power position of the other (honor/pride). In this sense, the whole performance of everyday racism can be seen as a re-actualization of history, placing Kathleen back in a colonial order where she experiences dishonor and shame.

Suddenly colonialism is experienced as real – one feels it! This *immediacy*, in which the past becomes present and the present, the past, is another characteristic of classic trauma. One experiences the present as if one were in the past. On the one hand, colonial scenes (the past) are restaged through everyday racism (the present), and on the other hand, everyday racism (the present) restages scenes of colonialism (the past). The wound of the present is still the wound of the past, and vice versa; the past and present become interlocked as a result.

15. "WHAT BEAUTIFUL SKIN... I WANT TO BE A 'N.' ... TOO!" – ENVY AND DESIRE FOR THE BLACK SUBJECT

In Kathleen's episode, the girl not only invokes the process of dishonor and shame; she also reveals a desire to be Black. She contemplates the Black female body and admits wanting to become Black, to have a Black body too: "[T]he beautiful eyes that the 'Negerin' has! And the beautiful skin (...) I want to be a 'Negerin' too!" she declares.

Racism emerges here in the form of passion for 'the exotic' and 'the primitive.' Kathleen's body is celebrated and enjoyed, but nevertheless in the realm of primitivism. This desire to become Black or desiring Blackness is deeply embedded in the fantasy that racial 'Others' are closer to nature and authenticity, and therefore have access to something *whites* have lost (hooks 1992). Black people become the representation of what society has pushed aside and designated dangerous, threatening and forbidden. Such projections, however, are the dimensions that make life exciting and vivid. These projections thus come to form the basis of primarily unconscious racial envy, where there is simultaneously a wish "to possess certain of the desired attributes of the Other at the same time that the Other must be destroyed because (she/he) represents something perceived as lacking in [the self]" (Sernhede 2000: 314). In the *white* conceptual world, in other words, the Black subject becomes an object of desire that must at the same time be attacked and destroyed.[33] Kathleen seems to be desired – she is an object of exoticism – but her position as an object of racial desire cannot be dissociated from the envy involved. At any moment, Kathleen can be transformed from a fascinating Black woman into a humiliated 'N.,' from an exotic woman into a *Scheißausländerin*,[34] from good into bad, from sweet into bitter – according to her *white* public's fears and desires.

---

33 During colonialism, racial rape and lynching were the cruelest examples of this envy. Rape and the act of possessing and violating the Black female body were common practices, as was the lynching of Black men accused of having had sexual relations with *white* women or merely having spoken to, whistled at or tried to approach them. The Black body is simultaneously sexually desired and physically destroyed.

34 *T. fucking foreigner.*

Moreover, the girl refers exclusively to the body – the skin and the eyes – perceiving Kathleen at the level of the body, 'absolutely as the not-self' (Fanon 1967: 161). Fanon uses Lacan's schema of the mirror stage to explain why in the *white* world Black people are reduced to a body. When one has grasped the mechanism described by Lacan, writes Fanon, "one can have no further doubt that the real other for the *white* man is and will continue to be the black man" (1967: 161). The Black subject is used as a counterpart for the *white* subject, as a mirror image that is reduced to physicality. We are perceived as images of bodies – the dancers, singers, performers, and athletes of *white* arenas.

16. "YOU GET THIS ACHE IN YOUR FINGERS" – THE UNSPEAKABLE PAIN OF RACISM

And then... then... I remember feeling for the first time... this kind of physical pain because someone called me that word. You get this ache in your fingers, there is something... I never felt that before in my body... That was the very first time, I mean, I vaguely remember one time when someone called me '*Negerin,*' when I was very little, and that was it.

It was precisely the sound of the *N*-word, and the whole agonizing meaning behind it, that shocked and alarmed Kathleen. I speak of 'alarm' because the word so efficiently expresses the horrors of racism, recalling pain that again describes the concept of trauma. Kathleen repeatedly hears a word that has historically classified and positioned her as 'an inferior race,' as an abused and excluded subject. Even though – or even because – it is a child speaking, the symbolic violence of the *N*-word does not vanish or fade away.

Apparently the pain exposed on the body is the expression of the internal wound caused by the violence of the *N*-word: as Kathleen says, she felt "this kind of physical pain because someone called [*her*] that word." This is an interesting parallelism: racism intends to damage the Black subject (*schlecht machen*) and the Black subject indeed feels physically damaged (*sich schlecht fühlen*). One is 'badly' injured and one feels 'bad.' The need to transfer the psychological experience of racism onto the body conveys the idea of trauma in the sense of an unspeakable experience, a dehumanizing event, to which one does not have adequate words or symbols to respond. One is often speechless. The need to transfer the psychological experience of racism onto the body – the soma – can be seen as a form of protecting the self by pushing the pain to the 'outside' (somatization).

The experience of racism, because is so horrifying, cannot actually be grasped cognitively and assigned meaning; rather "it remains unprocessed – not 'knowledge' in the usual sense, yet felt in the body" (Kaplan 1999: 147). The agony of racism is therefore expressed through bodily sensations, urged to the outside and written on the body. The language of trauma is, in this sense, physical, graphic and visual, articulating the incomprehensible effect of pain. "(T)his kind of physical pain" and "the ache on your fingers" related by Kathleen visually illustrate the traumatic violence and loss involved in the experience of everyday racism.

Being called 'N.' also reminds Kathleen of her vulnerability among *whites* who can play with the brutality of the African holocaust whenever they want to. Whiteness then becomes a signal of threat or terror. As bell hooks writes, Black people always "live with the possibility that they will be terrorized by Whiteness" (1995: 46), making the association of whiteness with terror. This terrifying violence, however, is mostly expressed in subtle ways. As Philomena Essed argues, "We recognize racism most easily when it is expressed in outward and direct ways. Experience has shown that Whites often consciously or unconsciously conceal their own racist intentions in their contact with Blacks. This in turn can make it difficult for Blacks to point to discriminatory treatment in a given situation" (1990: 33). I thus reformulate a sentence I wrote before: the game of sweet and bitter words not only makes it difficult to identify racism; the game of sweet and bitter words IS a form of producing racism. The difficulty of identifying racism is not only functional for racism, but also a very part of racism itself.

17. "EVERYBODY IS DIFFERENT (...) AND THAT MAKES THE WORLD GREAT..." – THE THEATRE OF RACISM AND ITS TRIANGULATION

The girl's mother, first of all she was very embarrassed and she was trying to talk about how everybody is different and how wonderful that is... and I don't remember exactly what she said, I didn't quite understand her. My friend translated for me later and said she was talking about how everyone is different, there are Black people, there are Jews too, and that's what makes the world great, something like this... I remember that my friend didn't know what to do either... and... I don't know... er... I don't know what I did to get over that.

Kathleen describes the core scenario of racism, the framework in which racism is played out and where each player has a very specific role: the *white* girl as the one who insults, Kathleen as the singled-out Black woman, the insulted; and the *white* mother and the *white* boyfriend as the 'silent' observers. It is the typical *triangular* constellation of racism. I call it triangular because of its three characters and the three different functions they have that make racism possible: first, the actor who performs racism; second, the Black subject who becomes the object of racial aggression; and finally, the consensus of the *white* audience observing the performance.

This constellation reminds me of Frantz Fanon's classic episode in which the boy next to his mother expresses his racial fears of the Black man, insulting him: "Mama, a Negro!..." "Take no notice, sir, he does not know that you are as civilized as we..." (1967: 113), says the mother to Fanon. "Look how handsome that Negro is!" (1967: 114) she tells her son, pointing at Fanon. In Kathleen's narrative, the little girl's mother points at Kathleen, explaining how everybody is different and "that is wonderful." Such sympathetic comments cannot, however, erase the feeling of being 'dissected,' of having one's body "given back distorted" (Fanon 1967: 113), as one is being described with both contemplation and disdain. Fanon becomes a 'handsome negro,' just as Kathleen is a 'beautiful *N.*'– the game of sweet and bitter words.

Of course one could argue that the girl, still a child, is neither racist nor brutal; she is only curious and has no bad intentions. But why should Kathleen abruptly disappear from the scenario so that one may speak of the girl instead? How does the main character become suddenly peripheral and the *white* girl very central? Isn't this arrangement, in which *whites* are placed at the center and Blacks at the margins as unspoken subjects, characteristic of racism? And why does it seem easier to empathize with the insolent *white* girl than with the Black woman who was insulted? We should also ask whether those who are busy protecting the girl are not actually protecting themselves, considering that what the child says is part of what her own parents say.

This scene depicts the 'race'-gender relation and the power asymmetry between Black women and *white* women. Kathleen is an adult Black woman, who is being first insulted by a *white* child and then exposed and taught by the *white* mother in front of the *white* man. The coming together of the *white* girl, the *white* mother and the objectified Black woman, all before the *white* male, raises issues related to racial authority and gender. Moreover, in this constellation, the observers are special observers, as the mother is trying to educate her own daughter. She explains to her that "there are Black people, there are Jews too" – a dishonorable situation for Kathleen, who is first an object of *white* contempt and insult, and then an object of education, with which the little girl should learn about the people of the world. In both roles, Kathleen is serving the *white* spectators, who profit regardless of her presence. Servitude is perplexingly imposed upon Kathleen.

The use of such '*multi-kulti*' arguments – "everybody is different and that's what makes the world great" – supports the little girl's view that it must be indeed 'great' to be a '*N.*' Here, differences among people are being explained in aesthetic terms, and not in political terms. The little girl learns that racial 'Others' become different because they look different, not because they are treated differently. The enunciation of difference is constructed in a way that assumes that racialized groups are a pre-existing occurrence rather than a consequence of racism. As a result the girl is taught that people are discriminated against because they are different, when in fact it is the other way around: people become different through processes of discrimination. Kathleen is not a '*N.*' because of her Black body, but she becomes one through racist discourses that are fixed on the color of her skin.

CHAPTER 10

SEGREGATION AND RACIAL CONTAGION

18. "*WHITES* ON ONE SIDE, BLACKS ON THE OTHER"– RACIAL SEGREGATION AND *WHITE* FANTASIES OF RACIAL CONTAGION

> I grew up in a place called Y. It is not a big town and it feels like a small town (...) The town is divided, there is East Y and West Y. East Y is where most of the Black people live and West Y is where *white*s live, sort of... There is East Franklin street and West Franklin street... I think that's right... it might even be the other way around, I am not sure who's on the West and who's on the East, but there is a clear division... *white*s on the one side, Blacks on the other. That is where I was raised.

Describing the town where she grew up, Kathleen speaks of a division, a geographical boundary separating Blacks from *white*s. Visually, her town can be perceived in terms of 'race,' and 'race' can be used as a geographical orientation or even as a landmark, where each group has 'its own place.' The need to regulate the physical distance to Blacks and define the areas they can use reveals a very important dimension of everyday racism related to fantasies of racial contagion.

Black segregated areas represent places where *white*s care not to – or dare not – go and to which they maintain a particular corporeal distance. In describing this physical distance, David Marriott (1998) speaks of "*white* racial fears and anxieties about somatic contagion." The East- and West-side division Kathleen mentions is a geographical reminder of the borders the Black subject cannot transgress, so as not to contaminate *white* territory. Such geography exposes a power asymmetry in which *white*ness defines its own area and Blackness is confined to an area thus defined by *white*ness. This was the principal function of segregationist ideology, to confine racial 'Others.'

The resulting geographical division can be seen as a border or membrane between the world of the 'superiors' and the world of the 'inferiors,' between the 'acceptable' and the 'unacceptable,' the 'good' and the 'bad,' the 'We' and the 'Others,' preventing the first from an eventual contagion of the second. Symbolically, this membrane, separating both worlds, reminds me of the white gloves Black people were often forced to use when touching the *white* world – a thin and fine piece of material that functioned as medical prevention against somatic contagion. The white gloves were like a membrane, a border that physically separated the Black hand from the *white* world, protecting *white*s from being eventually infected by Black skin – for in the *white* imaginary, Black skin represented the 'inferior,' the 'unacceptable,' the 'bad,' the 'dirty' and the diseased. The *white*ness of the gloves masqueraded the Black hands and the Black skin of the hands was hidden behind the whiteness of the gloves. A perverse situation: the gloves protected *white*s from their primary fear of racial contagion and at the same time prevented Blacks from touching *white*s' privileges.

The idea of a membrane that contains or restricts Blackness becomes real in self-contained Black neighborhoods, where Blacks are placed on the outside, in marginal areas, prevented from having contact to *white resources* and goods. This ghettoization was created to foster the political control and economic exploitation of Blacks. So what happens when the Black subject crosses this membrane and enters *white* spaces?

19. "THE NEIGHBORHOOD WHERE I WAS LIVING WAS *WHITE*" – CROSSING THE BOUNDARIES AND HOSTILITY

The neighborhood where I was living was *white*, all of them were *white*. I remember one Black neighbor we had, it was a couple, they lived two blocks away from us, they had a beautiful house, had a yard that they kept perfect, it was a perfect yard! I remember that (...) It was a *white* settlement!... Yeah! I had a friend, a childhood friend, we are still very good friends now. This was the other Black family there... (*laughs*) Well, her mother, she is a professor of psychology at the university, and her family was a professional Black family whom we were in contact with (...) But they were really the only other Black family, I think, we could relate to. We could relate to them on a class level and we could relate to them also on a racial level.

Kathleen speaks of isolation. She describes a constellation in which her own and another Black family were positioned as solo in the *white* collective – as she says, apart from these two Black families, 'all of them were *white*.' The constellation in which Black people are positioned as solo is an arrangement resulting from segregation and therefore an expression of racism; the isolation of Black people is a strategy to reassure *white* dominance. Like in a triangulation, the Black subject has to be singled out in order not to dismantle the *white* consensus: one Black person is suitable and even interesting, two is a crowd. In this sense, isolation announces racism: all of them were *white* because most Blacks could not enter. They were kept 'in their place,' barred from 'taking their place.'

Such racial isolation exposes how little access Black people have to so-called 'integrated neighborhoods' that offer better living and educational conditions. "Where can you see Black people? And where not?" Housing segregation based on 'race' does exist in Europe.[35] Black people who are exposed to a large majority of *white*s, writes Philomena Essed, "are aware of the hostile sentiments among some neighbors, who are reluctant to accept Blacks on 'their' street" (1991: 216). Kathleen's description enables us to recognize that, despite being in a *white* environment, she seems not to have had close contact or access to her *white* neighbors; they are described as an anonymous mass, in opposition to the Black families, especially when she speaks of her childhood friend. This lack of closeness with dominant group members is common, argues Philomena Essed (1991), since *white* neighbors often avoid or withdraw from social contact with nearby Black residents.

Isolation reveals how the lives of Black people are shaped by an introjected anxiety of being attacked by *white* fears of contagion. In psychoanalytical terms anxiety responds exactly to some as of yet unrecognized factors: *Why are so few Black people here? What could that signify? Am I safe here?* One cannot avoid associating one's own isolation with the *white* fear of being contaminated by Blackness and, consequently, with an introjected fear that one might be attacked, as one is phantasmally perceived as 'dirt' in 'their' territory.

The idea of dirt is related to order. Dirty means anything that is not in the right place. Implicitly, things are not dirty in themselves, but they become as such when positioned in a system of ordering that has no place for them. A spoon placed on a serving dish or a saucer, for instance, is not seen as dirty, but it becomes dirty when it is placed on the table, soiling the table and its tablecloth. Physically the spoon itself has not changed, but the ordering has changed; it is said that the spoon belongs on the saucer, so as soon as the spoon touches the table, it is no longer in the right place and is said to be dirty. Just like the Black hands, they are clean and 'in their place' – serving – as long as masqueraded by the white gloves, otherwise they are perceived as 'dirty.' This schema of cleanliness versus dirtiness and place within a system of ordering, according to Mary Douglas (1966, quoted in Mecheril 2000),

---

35 In the United States, it is common for housing agencies to use quotas to determine the maximum percentage of Blacks allowed in a neighborhood. It is implicitly assumed that 'exposing' the *white* population to too many Blacks is unfair (Essed 1991).

can be used to understand racial segregation and the unwillingness to have Black people in *white* spaces. Those who are segregated against become seen as 'dirty' as soon as they transgress the system of ordering that places them as marginal. At the margins, they are not 'dirty,' but because the system does not provide a place for them as equals, they become infectiously dirty as soon as they enter the centre, where they are outside their order and therefore perceived as 'dirty.' In his essays, Paul Mecheril (2000) uses an aesthetic vocabulary to narrate exclusion and segregation. He speaks of the use of 'beauty' and 'ugliness' in the context of racial difference within the nation. Racial 'Others' and their presence are seen as the cause of 'national ugliness' because it is imagined that before their arrival the nation was 'beautiful.' But now the nation is 'ugly.' It is the presence of non-nationals in the nation, the non-We in the We space, that makes the nation ugly, disfiguring it, infecting it, dirtying it. This aesthetic schema of beauty and ugliness constructs differences between insiders and outsiders.

CHAPTER 11

PERFORMING BLACKNESS

20. "IF I WERE THE ONLY BLACK STUDENT IN THE CLASS, I HAD TO, IN A SENSE, REPRESENT WHAT THAT MEANT" – PERFORMING PERFECTION AND REPRESENTING THE 'RACE'

> I think I had a very positive experience as a child (...) My parents made sure to tell me I was very special (...) My father made sure that we could compete with everybody, with everybody! He never specifically said *white* people, *white* students... but I was surrounded by *white* people, it was quite clear what he meant with that. But it was very important to compete and to be competitive... and to stand out also. If I were the only Black student in the class, I had to, in a sense, represent what that meant. Represent that we were just as smart or if not even smarter than the others.

Kathleen becomes a representative of the 'race.' This status of having to represent Blackness announces racism: Kathleen has to represent those who are not there, and Black people are not there because their access to structures is denied. A circle of double inclusion and exclusion, it is precisely this position as singled out, as included in a space of exclusion, that turns Kathleen into an exemplar of her 'race': "I had to (...) represent what that meant." Being included always means representing the excluded, which is why we often find ourselves forced into the role of 'race' deputies. We come to represent all the others. Kathleen is therefore not only seen as *a* 'race,' but she also recognizes in herself the responsibility of being *the* 'race.'

This process of absolute identification – or essentialism – in which one is merely seen as a 'race' is only possible because within racism one is denied the right to subjectivity. Kathleen is not just Kathleen; she is a 'body,' she is a 'race,' she is a 'history.' She exists in this triplicity. Caught in this triple person, one has to be at least three times better than any *white* in order to become equal. While those in the class have the privilege of existing in the first person, Kathleen exists in the triple person. While *white* others speak as individuals, as Sally, Christine or John, Kathleen speaks as a body, as a 'race,' as a child of former slaves. She is given three places to represent. "(T)here were legends, stories, history, and above all historicity" about who one is, writes Fanon (1967: 112), and one comes to represent all of them. Fanon describes his triple existence, as he becomes responsible for his own body, for his own 'race,' and for his ancestors, just like Kathleen. Whatever room she enters, she is never the self, but the entire group – a group subjected to severe examination. "I was battered down by tom-toms, cannibalism, intellectual deficiency, fetishism, racial defects, slave-ships," concludes Fanon. He calls this a 'racial epidermal schema' (1967: 112), one that shatters the Black subject into a triple person. It is not a 'bodily schema,' but a 'racial schema,' inscribed on the skin, that guides us through space. Memories, legends, jokes, comments, stories, myths, experiences, insults, all of them symbolically inscribed on the surface of our skin, telling us where to sit and where not to sit, where to go and where not to go, whom to talk with and whom not to talk with. We move in space, in alert, through this racial epidermal schema: "I was surrounded by *white* people," says Kathleen. "It was quite clear what (my father) meant with that."

There is another dimension described by Kathleen. Not only does she have the responsibility of representing the 'race,' – a 'race' embodied by negative connotations – she also has to defend it. Since racism is a regime that is discursive and not biological, such equivalences – lack of wisdom, lack of culture, lack of history, lack of language, lack of intelligence – become accepted. In this sense, Kathleen is not a simple schoolgirl in a classroom; she is an observed Black schoolgirl imprisoned in racialized images that she has to oppose every day. She has to make sure that she can prove "we were just as smart or if not even smarter than the (*white*) others."

> I got used to being singled out, I got used to being the only Black person at all in my classes. And most of the time I was. I was in all these honors classes, I was in advancement placement classes, I was getting college credits even before I graduated from my school, and I was in the honor society, I was in all kinds of organizations, I was in all the kinds of things that I knew would get me ahead, in terms of my education (...) I got very accustomed to being the only (Black) person in these classes... and those people in those classes also get very used to me being the only Black person there, and that was OK with them. I wasn't aware that there were certain things that people used to say to me, that I never acknowledged was racism. Ah!... things like... "You're Black but (...)" And then you can fill the blank with whatever you want to... "Even though you're Black (...)" Everything was... For some reason I was not like the other Black kids. For some reason I was Black, but still approachable, I was still OK. I was smart... but... I was especially smart (despite) being Black. It was always something... Being Black was always something on the side, that had to be placed somewhere, it was never really... I never felt it... it was never integrated in what I was. It was maybe what people call 'positive racism' in a sense, I don't

know... or exoticism... but I wouldn't really call it that way because it is still... racism.

Kathleen is defined as a 'race,' and at the same time, the 'race' is dissociated from her because she is smart. She is Black, *but* smart. The 'but' is the dissociative element. It dissociates smartness from Blackness, turning both into two categories that contradict one another. To repair such massive dissociation, we indeed often see ourselves forced to associate both with excellence, forced to give an excellent performance of ourselves, an excellent performance of Blackness. We become excellent actors of our competences: not mediocre, not common, not average, but excellent. "I was in all these honors classes, I was in advancement placement classes, I was getting college credits even before I graduated from my school..." explains Kathleen, emphasizing her Blackness and her smartness as two associated categories.

The ego defense mechanism of *dissociation* allows two or more mental processes to co-exist without becoming connected or integrated; that is, the different parts of a subject are not combined into a whole. Smartness and Blackness co-exist as separate categories, as alienated parts of Kathleen, but not as integral parts of her. In this sense, Kathleen is acknowledged as smart like *whites*, but Black like the others outside. "You're Black, but..." she explains. She is smart as long as she is being compared to whiteness; consequently Blackness is always "something on the side." Her skin is described as both primary and accessory. One is Black, 'but' one is not. One is Black when it comes to embodying the corporeal, but one is not Black when it comes to intellect. One is Black when it comes to embodying stupidity, but one is not Black when it comes to embodying wisdom. One is Black when it comes to embodying the negative, but one is likewise *white* when it comes to embodying the positive. What hallucinatory thoughts, for the *white* subject to believe we are not really Black when we are good, but indeed Black when we are bad – what a *white* hallucination!

21. "BUT WHERE DO YOUR GREAT-GRANDPARENTS COME FROM?" – COMING TO GERMANY

I came to Germany. I read this book *Farbe bekennen*,[36] I was reading about Black Germans and felt a certain affinity with the idea of grow-

---

36 The book *Farbe bekennen* (T. *Showing Our Colors*), as previously mentioned, is an anthology of narratives written by Afro-German women describing their experiences as

ing up in a *white* community and being isolated. It was a shock to find out that actually my experience was far less extreme than a lot of Black people in this country who grow up being the only Black persons in the family, I mean that is... Oh, god! (...) And always being asked to explain how come one is German, even though one is Black. I mean, this is an experience I went through many times... of being asked... but because I speak English, they ask me instead when do I intend to leave and they try to trace me back to Africa, yes... to trace me back.

When I was giving English classes, there was this class... well, I think they were not very educated people, anyway... a couple of women wanted to know where do I come from, and I said: "I am from the USA." And they asked, "Yes, but your parents?" and I said, "From the USA!" And they kept asking: "Yes, but your grandparents, where are your grandparents from? And your great-grandparents?" And I answered: "From the US!" And that never stopped... (*laughs*) They asked me until they could trace me back to Africa. "Ah! You're from Africa!" "No. My ancestors are from Africa. I am from the US." "Yes, from Africa!" (*laughs*). The sad part of it is that they do not take in consideration our history. I do know that my ancestors are African, but that's all... the system of slavery did not allow us either to know where we were brought from or who we were: We lost our names, our languages... I mean, we were sold by *white* slavers to *white* people... It is, of course, insulting when they ask, "But where in Africa?"

There are two important moments within this episode. The first is the moment of being placed outside the *white* nation – being asked when one intends to leave because one's 'race' does not belong 'here' – while the second relates to the history of slavery – being asked where one comes from, even though this information was never allowed to be known. Kathleen is being questioned by *white* people about a part of her history that *whites* themselves banned. It is this second moment, a moment of double estrangement, which I would like to explore here.

Neither the *white* women nor Kathleen know where Kathleen's ancestors came from, but they do not know for different reasons. While the *white* women do not know because they do not have to know, Kathleen does not

---

Black women in a *white*-dominated society. The book was edited by Katharina Oguntoye, Dagmar Schulze and May Ayim, the last of whom died by suicide in 1996. Later in the interview Kathleen expresses her interest in the work of May Ayim and her suicide.

know because 'not having the right to know' was an integral part of slavery politics. 'Not knowing' would erase the enslaved African as a subject with history. In other words, Kathleen does not know, not because she does not care, but because she was denied access to her history. There was a fracture, a rupture, that deliberately separated her from parts of her history: Where were we brought from? Who were we? Which names? Which languages? Because the information was erased, these are questions that will remain unanswered. "(A)nd that is the sad part of it," as Kathleen argues. "(T)he sad part of it is that they do not take in consideration our history." Kathleen is disturbed by the idea that those who ask are not aware of the content of their questions. They are asking for what they have symbolically concealed – her history. The questions embody the fantasy that we all have access to our collective historical biography, whether colonizer or colonized, master or slave. Such a fantasy is only possible if history has been forgotten – that is, if they are suffering from historical amnesia. But how can four hundred very recent years of history be forgotten? How can one not remember? This seems to be Kathleen's concern: "I mean, we were sold by *white* slavers to *white* people." How could they have forgotten? And how dare they ask, in order to be reminded? "It is, of course, insulting when they ask."

The past returns in the form of intrusive questions: "But your grandparents, where are your grandparents from? And your great-grandparents?" The intrusiveness of these questions resides in the fact that they invoke a traumatic past of rupture and loss, a past that still defines those of the African Diaspora as fractured identities. This reveals how the past is intimately bound to the present. Slavery and its legacy are present in Kathleen's current biography. As Kathleen says, "I do know that my ancestors are African, but that's all." The past therefore co-exists with the present, and the memory of slavery is part of the present. This sense of timelessness is a characteristic of classic trauma.

22. "FOREIGNERS HAVE IT BETTER HERE THAN PRISIONERS" – RACIST CONFESSIONS AND AGGRESSION

I had taught a class, every Monday I taught a class of a company called AMP in Berlin. And that was a class of four women, four secretaries, all of them *white*, and I think one was from the West and three were from the East – which actually doesn't matter for what I am going to tell. And one day, I don't remember how we got into the topic, but I was asking them about... Oh! About foreigners coming to Germany

(...) And they started saying things that were incredible, I couldn't believe it... I was standing in front of them, obviously a foreigner, and they were still comfortable enough to say these things. This was part of the thing that came from my town, people were always comfortable enough to expose their racism because they didn't... they thought they were safe with me. And the *white* German women started telling me how there are too many foreigners here, the laws are much too soft, and foreigners have it better here than prisoners, and... all kinds of things coming out. And one woman at the end told me, "Well, I hope these things don't surprise you, most of the people think this way! Most people feel like we do..." And at the end of the class I felt... I felt like a dog, I just couldn't think... I mean it was horrible, you can imagine...

This situation of indirect racist insult is violent because it exposes hatred toward Blacks as if one were not Black – as if one did not belong to the group being insulted. Paul Mecheril describes this process of using a third group to express racism as a *categorical experience of racism* (1998): categorical in that Kathleen is being put in the category of *foreigner*. Because Kathleen is a 'foreigner,' she will always be insulted each time the group 'foreigners' is insulted. In other words, when devaluating speeches about 'foreigners' are made, Kathleen is being inferred without being referred to in person. This form of expressing racism toward Black people is alienating because one is being insulted without being the direct object of insult. It is not the second, but the third person being used; it is not 'you,' but 'they,' even though both coincide and become one.

But this dynamic defines one dimension of everyday racism. Because one is there and one is Black, racism is performed using those who are not there and Black as the direct characters. It is precisely because of one's presence that the *white* public performs racism toward those who are not there, to warn us of how they perceive us. This makes it difficult to identify racism because one is being simultaneously included and excluded: "(P)eople were always comfortable enough to expose their racism because they (...) thought they were safe with me," says Kathleen. The comfort, however, is not because Kathleen personally offers them any relief; it is rather because of this simultaneous inclusion and exclusion that makes the *white* public comfortable enough to perform racism.

The Black subject is told to be simultaneously equal and different – equal in the sense that Kathleen is a confidant for the *white* women, and different because she is the object of hate in their confessions – an alienating situation for the Black woman who is simultaneously placed as the self and as 'Other.' The presupposition in such situations is that the Black woman must consider it a compliment that the *white* group does not reject her, but instead rejects the 'Others.' So one is included while one's own racial group is excluded, and it is this individual inclusion within a collective exclusion that is expected to be seen as flattering. Kathleen, however, does not feel flattered at all, but shocked: "I felt like a dog, I just couldn't think..." She starts describing the idea of an unexpected shock – "they told me incredible things" – and then shifts to the idea of isolation and separation, caused by a traumatic shock. The metaphor "like a dog" expresses this sense of separation, as dogs are not humans.

Dogs are not humans, and prisoners are humans who have committed a crime against humanity. The remark "foreigners have it better here than prisoners" communicates outrageous fantasies. Because those who have committed a crime are not dignifying members of a society, the association between 'foreigners' and 'criminals' reveals the construction of foreignness as threatening and undignified. The association therefore indicates the place where these women fantasize keeping 'foreigners' – in prison, away from *white* society. In such fantasies, foreigners come to occupy a more dishonorable position than criminals themselves. The *white* women express their belief that the first group does not deserve to live as well as the second. To their annoyance, 'foreigners' are indeed better off than criminals. Criminals and prisoners are supposedly fantasized here as being both *white* and nationals, in opposition to the 'foreigners.' And in this sense, the women's annoyance consists of the fact that some 'foreigner' is better off than a *white* criminal.

Within this constellation both the aggressors and the target of aggression are women. The *white* women, however, are in solidarity, not with the Black woman, but with *white* prisoners. 'Race' seems to be more important than gender, for in this constellation the *white* women express their empathy for We, the *white* Germans, and not We, women in general. It is the category of foreigners, both women and men, that is addressed with antipathy, a category that includes the woman Kathleen. Kathleen is seen as a 'foreigner,' not as a woman. Such experiences explain why Black women describe their experiences of oppression first in relation to 'race' rather than gender, as our exploitation is primarily based on racial aspects and can be personified by *white* females.

23. "MY MOTHER COMMITTED SUICIDE (...) I THINK SHE WAS VERY LONELY IN OUR TOWN" – RACISM, ISOLATION AND SUICIDE

In 1992 my mother committed suicide, and that was just before my last year of high school. She was in her early forties when she did it, and I think she was also... I think she was very lonely in our town. She didn't have many friends at all. I remember there were times when she told me I was the only friend she had, which I didn't believe because I was only ... I was her daughter. But she didn't have a social circle. I think my mother was very isolated and I think she was aware of what it was about (...) I think she couldn't... she was in a *white* environment, and she did not like it at all. She hated mixing and pretending... she wasn't an integrationist, let's put it that way... *(laughs)*. Well, she didn't have any problems having *white* friends or something, she wasn't separate, but she needed to be reflected in the society where she was, and she simply wasn't. Not where she worked, she worked at the university, where most were *white* people there; my father's social circle was always *white*, his colleagues, the university professors as well... and that was difficult for my mother. She always felt she had to perform when she was operating in my father's social circles.

Kathleen relates her mother's suicide to racism and isolation. This is a powerful association, the connection between racism and death, as suicide can effectively be portrayed as racism's assassination of the self. Within racism, suicide is almost the visualization, the performance of the Black subject's condition in a *white* society: one is made invisible, and this invisibility is performed through the realization of suicide. A painful sequence, but a very realistic one: "(S)he needed to be reflected in the society," says Kathleen, "and she simply wasn't." Because racism forces one to exist as 'Other,' depriving the Black subject of a proper self, suicide can indeed be seen as an act of performing one's own imperceptible existence. In other words, one acts the loss of self by murdering the place of Otherness.

Kathleen was not the only interviewee to reveal a story of suicide in the family. Two other Black women did as well: one who had lost her mother and a second who had lost a close girl-friend. In a process of free association, both made a strong connection between racism, isolation and suicide, just like Kathleen. In slave and colonial narratives, there are a large number of accounts connecting suicide to the impact of racism and isolation. Toni Morrison, for instance, based her novel *Beloved* on the true story of Margaret Garner, an enslaved woman in the US, who, after escaping from the plantation and being found by her *white* slave owner, attempted to kill her four children and herself. The idea of returning to the plantation as a slave – as the 'Other' of whiteness – was so horrifying that she tried to kill her children and herself in front of the *white* master. Before she was caught, she succeeded in killing one child, who actually becomes the main character in Morrison's novel, the infant daughter Beloved. It was, however, the shocking condition of existing as the 'Other' of the *white* subject that led Garner to attempt to kill herself and her children. "I'm a human being. These are my children," declared Garner in an interview for a local newspaper. Her intended suicide and infanticide were a form of protecting herself and her children from a system of slavery that dehumanized them and removed them from the realm of selfhood.

In this sense, suicide can also emerge as an act of becoming a subject. Deciding not to live under the *white* master's conditions is a final performance in which the Black subject claims subjectivity. In the context of slavery, Black communities were collectively punished every time one of their members attempted or committed suicide. This brutal reality emphasizes the subversive function of suicide within racial oppression. The punishment upon the enslaved community reveals, of course, the interest of the *white* masters in not losing 'property,' but above all, it reveals an interest in preventing enslaved Africans from becoming subjects. Suicide performs autonomy, as only a subject can decide about her/his own life or determine her/his existence.

And I think all of that played a role in her choice to end her life... After I left my town, a year later... I went to college, and that was really the first time that I found myself in a community, with Black students and people of color. That was the first time that I could say: "I can name racism! I can name internalized racism! Institutionalized racism!" Suddenly I found out that all these things had a name, and I recognized patterns. I could say: "Yes, that's what is happening with me too!" I could name everything suddenly... and also I could apply a sort of logic to the why of my mother's death, that I hadn't been able before (...) In a way there was no space for her there as a Black woman, she couldn't find herself reflected there... and there were so many invisible barriers that she couldn't have passed, I mean she just couldn't...

In a gender-'race' schema, however, this state of Otherness is more complex, as Kathleen's words explain. Being neither *white* nor men, Black women come to occupy a very difficult position within *white* supremacist patriarchal society. We represent a kind of a double lack, a double Otherness, as we are the antithesis of both whiteness and masculinity.

In this schema, the Black woman can only be 'Other,' and never the self. "My father's social circle was always *white*, his colleagues, the university professors as well... and that was difficult for my mother," explains Kathleen. Her father, as a Black male, could operate in both *white* male and *white* female circles, but not her mother, who was a Black female. She could only be the 'Other' of Otherness. As Lola Young writes, a Black woman inevitably "serves as the other of others without sufficient status to have an other of her own" (1996: 100). White women have an oscillating status, as the self and as 'Other' to *white* men because they are *white,* but not male; Black men serve as opponents for *white* males as well as potential competitors for *white* women because they are men, but not *white;* Black women, however, are neither *white* nor male, and serve as the 'Other' of Otherness.

In this context of absolute isolation, suicide among Black women can be seen as the perfection of their existence as the 'Other' of others: perfectionism in the sense that suicide is the 'perfect' portrayal of a disqualified self, a self that has no 'Other' of its own – a faultless act of non-existence.

24. "THE GREAT MOTHERS OF THE BLACK 'RACE'" – THE 'SUPER STRONG BLACK WOMAN' AND THE SILENT SUFFERING

I always get very angry when people, especially Black women, celebrate the strength of the Black woman and the legendary image of the dark-skinned superwoman. I constantly hear how Black women don't commit suicide because they are too busy being the Great Mothers of the Black Race. Suicide and therapy are only for lazy, self-pitying *white* women who have nothing better to do with their time and money. I remember hearing a Black woman telling me very bluntly that Black women do not commit suicide because they simply don't have the time: they have children, jobs, and so many other things to take care of that they have no time to consider killing themselves. I wanted very badly to tell her that my experience had taught me otherwise, but the stereotype of the superstrong Black woman is so overwhelmingly present.

The idea of the 'dark-skinned superwoman,' to use Kathleen's term, can on the one hand be seen as a political strategy to overcome negative representations of Black women in the *white* world; on the other hand, it imprisons Black women in an idealized image that does not allow us to express the profound wounds of racism. Kathleen speaks of this ambivalence, of having to fulfill empowering images – images that may actually be experienced as disempowering in that they silence the psychological damage of everyday racism.

In the 1960s, the Black feminist movement invested in images of the 'powerful Black woman' and the 'super-strong Black matriarch.' These images emerged in response to racist representations of the Black woman as lazy, submissive and neglectful of their children (Collins 2000; hooks 1992; Reynolds 1997). Vigorous and hard-working instead of lazy, assertive and independent instead of submissive, devoted instead of neglectful, such political images were a form of claiming a new identity. This is particularly visible in Black literature and philosophies, argues Patricia Hill Collins (2000), where the Black woman and the image of the Black matriarch have been tendentiously glorified, especially by Black men – in honor of their mothers, but unfortunately not of their wives. The images are richly endowed with the idea of strength, self-sacrifice, dedication and unconditional love – attributes that are associated with the archetype of motherhood, but which inadvertently refuse to acknowledge the real Black female experience.

It is the ability to survive under the adverse conditions of gendered racism that is being praised in these images. However, the portrait of the strong Black woman has been used in the *white* public to confirm old racist stereotypes. In her essay about the *(mis)representation of the Black (super) woman*, Tracey Reynolds (1997) reflects upon how the image of the strong, single and independent Black woman has been effectively adopted by the media to construct the Black male as pathologically absent, unreliable and sexually irresponsible, and the Black family as a destroyed 'institution.' This form of media attention, she argues, is divisive and contentious, creating hostilities between Black women and Black men, and effectively preventing a forum for debating the impact of racism on gender constructions.

I remember another woman (...) once used the example of a woman in Mozambique who managed to give birth to her child in a tree during the flood last year as proof of how tough we are: "No *white* woman could ever do that. *White* women run to therapists and psychologists when they have problems. Not us. We don't need all that." It hurts to hear these things, especially coming from other Black women, but at the same time, I feel that there is nothing I can say to challenge it. Maybe my mother would have benefited from some sort of counseling, if there had been appropriate resources available to her. I don't think that we are ever taught to recognize when we need help, I know of so many [Black] women who have been overcome by depression at some point in their lives (...)

I was talking with this woman yesterday. We were talking about this strength and this power image... and she was telling me how she felt that the thing that *white* people in Germany hate about Black women is that strength. They fear our strength, and they fear our power, and they fear the strength that they cannot control. On one hand, I think I understood what she was saying, but on the other hand, I thought: "I'm not any stronger than any other *white* woman out there who is at least my size!" But I would like to be seen... there's also nothing gratifying about being another stereotype. About being seen as this woman of steel, who's got this strength... this strength is not always there, there are times when I feel so weak (...) When I am angry, I want to have the freedom of being angry, and when I am weak I would like to have the freedom of being weak, without being taken advantage of. I don't want to be super-human anymore than I want to be sub-human.

After one is de-idealized, one becomes idealized, and behind this idealization lies the danger of a second alienation. In both processes one remains a response to a colonial order. The idealized images emerge as an inversion of the primary racist images: "(T)here's nothing gratifying about being another stereotype," says Kathleen, describing this process as doubly alienating. "I don't want to be super-human anymore than I want to be sub-human." Kathleen wants to be reflected in her complexity as both good and bad, strong and weak, bitter and sweet – that is, as a subject.

In the subtext of these controlling images, Black women only find themselves in the third person, as they speak about themselves through descriptions of *white* women. "*White* women run to therapists and psychologists when they have problems. Not us," says a woman to Kathleen. The woman speaks of a third person – a *white* woman – in order to describe herself, the first person. This third person is the norm and one is referring to oneself again through the *white* norm, describing the norm in order to expose one's peripheral position. "(L)azy, self-pitying *white* women who have nothing better to do with their time and money" describes the opposite social condition of Black womanhood: working hard, nursing and nurturing *white* families, having no lives of their own and existing in poverty. Thus the narration of racism takes place, through descriptions of the *white* other in binary oppositions: *white* woman/Black woman, lazy/hard-working, privileged/unprivileged, rich/poor. One term only gains meaning in relation to its counterpart.

CHAPTER 13

HEALING AND
TRANSFORMATION

25. "THOSE DOLLS, YOU SEE THEM IF YOU GO TO PLANTATION HOUSES IN THE SOUTH" – COLONIAL OBJECTS AND THE TRANSFORMATION OF SPACES

There was this Black figure, a Black boy doll that my neighbor had on her balcony... I and my roommate were trying to decide what we should do about it, if we should throw things at it or write anonymous letters and put them in her mail box... and one day I came home, I was just furious, and this woman happened to be on the balcony. I thought: "Today is the day!" I explained to her what the doll represented to me. I explained to her that a lot of those dolls, you see them if you go to plantation houses in the South (of the USA). *White* people put these little Black dolls, these little figures in front of the houses to greet people as they're coming in. She told me she thought it was cute...

Every day, when Kathleen leaves or enters her house, she is forced to see a Black figure that very unproblematically decorates her neighbor's balcony. This demonstrates how racist representations 'naturally' occupy public spaces and penetrate the private spheres of Black people, as Kathleen is forced to see the figure every day.

These Black figures appeared in the US in the post-slavery period as decorative objects for *white* households. Their appearance therefore coincides with both the abolition of slavery[37] and the physical absence of slaves from the plantations. In this context of political change, the Black figures emerged as personifications of slaves themselves, slaves who no longer existed. As decorative dolls, they came to occupy the 'exact place' enslaved Africans once had. As Kathleen explains to the *white* woman, "*(w)hite* people put these little Black dolls (...) in front of the houses to greet people as they're coming in," making the past an illusory present. The dolls thus personify a period of the past when Black people were considered sub-humans and treated inhumanly. With this in mind, one inevitably has to ask why *white* people are so keen on decorating their houses with slave dolls, slave lamps and so many other colonial objects. Why do these objects create so much aesthetic satisfaction? And why is it so important for the *white* subject to be surrounded by figurative slaves?

It seems that through such objects, the *white* subject recovers a resented *loss*. The loss of a good external object, the slave, is thus repaired by the Black

---

37 In the USA, slavery was officially abolished in 1865.

dolls, which come to substitute the former. They recreate the scenario of slavery, which the *white* subject persists in having. Suddenly it is as if Blacks were still there, 'in their place,' as dolls outside the entrance greeting the guests who have just arrived at the *white* household. Or as lamps, bearing light, while the *white* master reads a book. Or as ashtrays, to hold the ashes from the *white* master's cigarettes. Or as shoe shiners, to clean the *white* master's shit. The dolls personify both 'the place' Blacks have in the *white* imaginary and the secret *white* desire to own a slave. Why else would the *white* woman decorate her balcony with a Black doll? Isn't this a desire to recover what was lost?

Upon seeing the Black doll, Kathleen is reminded of 'the place' in which the *white* woman would like to have her. Racist representations have the double function of maintaining the *white* subject's fantasy that the 'Other' is still 'in her/his place,' and at the same time publicly announcing to the Black subject what 'her/his place' in society is. That is, they speak 'about' and 'to' the Black subject. The decorative figure speaks not only *about* Kathleen, but also *to* her by penetrating her space with a detrimental image of Blackness. Disturbed by the slave doll, which speaks about, Kathleen is captured in her thoughts of how to approach the woman who exhibits it: "(*We*) were trying to decide what we should do about it." Whether she wants to or not, Kathleen has to both face and oppose racism at the same time.

> After I explained to her what this figure represents, she said it was cute. And then she told me that her Cuban friend also thought it was cute. But I don't care about what her Cuban friend says. And I explained to her that there are three women of color living next door, and we thought it was a piece of shit, and all of our (*Black*) friends who are coming to visit us have to look at it too, and it was offensive to us, and it was invading our space, she was playing with something very serious, and if she's going to keep it on her balcony, she also needs to make sure that she knows that. Two weeks later she put a little plastic cover around it, I don't know if that was because of our conversation or not...

"(T)he doll is cute," says the neighbor to Kathleen. This process of infantilizing what the Black subject says prevents the *white* subject from acknowledging the reality of oppressed groups and therefore prevents her/him from looking at her/himself as an oppressor. "And then she told me that her Cuban friend also thought it was cute." Such banalization is a result of cognitive detachment, argues Philomena Essed; the "dominant group members do not understand, neither are they motivated to understand, the critique of Black women. This failure to understand and feel responsible for racism is legitimized by questioning the perspectives and personalities of opponents of racism" (1991: 272). That is what Kathleen's neighbor does by questioning Kathleen's perspective and telling her that even though she might find the Black doll problematic, her Cuban friend does not. He finds the doll cute, just as she does.

Interesting, however, is the triangulation the *white* woman constructs in order to validate her own opinion, a triangle that again positions Kathleen as singled out and the *white* woman as a collective, protected by a third person. The *white* other cannot face the Black subject in duo, but rather in trio; the need to get a third person and construct a triangle when speaking 'to' the Black subject reveals the threat we might represent in the *white* imaginary. This is not, however, a common triangulation where the third element coincides with the *white* consensus. This time, the third element is apparently a Black man or a man of color. The use of another Black person to invalidate Kathleen's knowledge about 'Black issues' is quite delicate, as the *white* woman is using a Black man to compete with a Black woman. This strategy reminds me of a process of colonial appropriation. The *white* woman confirms her power through the seizure of other Blacks, portraying a colonial dependency: *my Cuban friend also shares my opinion and he also does not have a problem with the Black doll.*

Interesting is how, in this episode, there are three Black figures. They could actually represent the developmental stages of racial history: the enslaved, represented by the Black boy doll; the assimilated, represented by the Cuban friend; and the racially aware Black woman, represented by Kathleen. From a gendered perspective, it is a constellation where the *white* woman possesses the 'Black boy' as well as the 'Black man,' who stands by the *white* woman. In this episode, the *white* woman can only deal with an infantilized, objectified and/or assimilated Black subject – assimilated in the sense of being as similar as possible to whiteness. Kathleen, however, is neither one nor the other. "(I told her) she was playing with something very serious, and if she is going to keep it in her balcony she also needs to make sure that she knows that." She is the speaking subject, transforming the space, as two weeks later, the doll is covered with plastic.

26. "I HAD TO READ A LOT, TO LEARN, TO STUDY (...) MEET OTHER BLACK PEOPLE." – DECOLONIZING THE SELF AND THE PROCESS OF DIS-ALIENATION

I also knew that all these names were wrong... but I couldn't explain why. And, of course, they will tell you that there is nothing wrong about them: "They don't mean what you think! They are neutral names... scientific." I had to read a lot, to learn, to study... I read many books... meet other Black people and realized they had experienced the same. So when I was able to define myself as Black and stopped calling myself all those awful names. Yes..!

Alicia describes how as a child she knew that the colonial terminology was 'wrong,' but she could not explain why. She used to hear that such terms didn't mean what she thought: "They are neutral...scientific." Alicia had to learn to define herself as politically Black. Alicia turns from the 'N.' to 'Mulata' (mule), to 'not Black at all,' to 'Mestiça' (mongrel dog) or to 'almost white,' according to the interests and fears of her *white* surrounding.

The terms *Schwarze/r*, *Afro-Deutsche*, and *Schwarze Deutsche* emerged as collective political self-definitions by Africans and African diasporic people in Germany (*Initiative Schwarze Menschen in Deutschland*).[38] These terms keep discriminatory colonial terminology at a distance while emphasizing the fact that those who have been constructed as 'M.', 'N.', 'M.' or 'M.' see themselves as a group and that this group even today occupies a position in society that, due to racism, is different from that of *whites* (Ayim 1997; Hügel-Marshal 2001; Oguntoye, Opitz and Schultz 1997).

In 1996 or 1997 I tried to talk with my adoptive mother about how racism affects my life. I gave her presents like the book *Farbe bekennen*, do you know this book? [*Yes!*] Or the essays and poetry books by May Ayim.[39] And my mother's brother, who is married with an Indian woman and has two children with her, said, "I think Alicia thinks too

---

38 *Initiative Schwarze Menschen in Deutschland* (*T.* Initiative of Black People in Germany) is an organization founded in the 1980s by Afro-Germans and Black people in Germany, which created a political and educational forum for dialogue, positive identification and Black consciousness.

39 May Ayim was a contemporary young Afro-German lyrical poetess, who in her essays wrote about being Black in Germany and her experience of isolation in a racialized society. She committed suicide in 1996.

much about racism, she's too busy with racism..." (*speaking with an intimidating and aggressive voice*). That's how it was living in a *white* family... racism was not allowed to be mentioned. And when I was twenty-one I told my parents not to use the word *Neger*, until then I was never able to talk about it... and they answered: "Oh, it's not a bad word! It means nothing bad!" The typical reaction... they simply said it is not a bad word, it is neutral, I am just too sensitive...

As an adult, Alicia offers her adoptive mother books that narrate the reality of racism in Germany. She offers the printed words of other Black women in order to sensitize her adoptive family to how racism affects her own life. The choice of books seems to protect her from eventual negations and trivialities because, unlike her own spoken words, printed words can be neither erased nor silenced.

When informed that Alicia reads such books, however, her uncle warns her about being 'too busy' with racism. His statement can be seen as a strategy *white* relatives have of protecting their Black children from becoming involved with the pain of racism by downplaying color as an issue and encouraging their Black children not to look at racism, as Tizard & Phoenix argue (1993). But to Alicia, it is a statement that prevents her from talking about her disconcerting experiences with the *white* world. Her uncle's words advise Alicia not to talk. His statement warns her that her engagement in reflecting upon racism is exaggerated, thus transmitting the idea that it is she who has a personal problem with racism. Racism is not a personal problem, but a structural and institutional *white* problem that Black people experience. This is a common occurrence for Black people when we bring up the issue of racism: intimidation on the one hand, individual pathologization on the other. Both are controlling mechanisms that prevent the *white* subject from hearing uncomfortable truths, which, if taken seriously, would ruin its power.

Yet, the fact that her uncle is married to an Indian woman and himself has children of color discourages Alicia and introduces another question: What function do Black children have for their *white* (adoptive) parents? This question, however, the interview material cannot answer.[40]

---

40   See Gaber & Aldridge (1994). *In the Best Interests of the Child: Culture, Identity and Transracial Adoption.* This book offers a complex view of the controversial discussion of transracial adoption.

27. "BLACK PEOPLE GREETED ME ON THE STREET..." – PIECING TOGETHER THE FRAGMENTS OF COLONIALISM

I think... since I was a child, every single time I saw a Black person on the street... they always greeted me, always. They look, smile or say hello, always... and keep walking. When I was little that used to disturb me a lot, people always looked and I didn't want to look back. But I never saw two Black people come across each other and not greeting, or at least looking at each other and smile, you know... We always greet ... I find it incredible. I don't know if other people do that, but I don't think so. Many times I look at Asian people, I observe them on the street to see if they greet, but they don't. Unless they know each other, otherwise they ignore each other. Or Arab people, for instance, they don't greet... They also don't greet, only if they know each other. From all people, Africans are the only ones who greet each other. Indian people also don't greet... maybe Native Americans greet, I don't know. We always greet. It's incredible, isn't it?... I think that has to do with our history, you know... we have such a special history, nobody has the history we have. We have been through centuries of discrimination and suffering, it is very deep...

Alicia describes how since she was a child, Black people have greeted her on the street: "they look, smile or say hello, always... and keep walking." This gesture, which she later associates with the particular history of African people, seems to re-create a union among those who greet one another.

People exchange greetings without knowing each other. The moment of salutation seems to be a collective ritual meant to repair the historical experience of rupture and fragmentation. In other words, the moment of greeting appears to be a process of reparation by which the individual recreates a link that has been broken. "I find it incredible," she adds, "(f)rom all people, Africans are the only ones who greet each other."

The Slave Trade has made Africa unique in its colonial history. While Slavery itself has existed since antiquity, and remains familiar in many different parts of the world, the Slave Trade was unique to African people in that for the first time in history, human beings became articles of trade; over centuries they could be bought, sold and replaced (Reed-Anderson 2000, Oguntoye 1997). Africa is the only continent whose population was traded: dismembered, enslaved, collectively segregated from society, and deprived of its rights, all for the profit of European economies.

The horrendous shock of separation and the violent pain of being deprived of one's link to the community, both within and outside the continent, are experiences of rupture that convey the classic definition of trauma. The dismembering of Africans emblematizes a colonial trauma. It is an occurrence that has tragically affected not only those who stayed behind and survived capture, but above all, those who were enslaved and taken abroad. Metaphorically, the continent and its peoples were disjointed, split and fragmented. It is this history of rupture that binds Black people all over the world.

Exchanging greetings can be seen as a collective ritual meant to repair this traumatic dismemberment, by bringing together those who have been split apart by force. It is primarily linked to the reparation of colonial trauma, and not necessarily to the experience of racism and its isolation; as Alicia recalls, many times she observed other people of color on the street who "don't greet, unless they know each other. (But) we always greet." The greeting relates to something that precedes the experience of everyday racism. Something leading back into history, a history of untainted fragmentation.

> For a long time I couldn't really understand what was behind this greeting, you know... When I was little it used to disturb me. When I got older (a teenager) I used to get upset, even though I was also curious. But I thought that was such an absurd... Why should they greet me?... 'Cause they didn't know me. Who do they think they are? I thought, just because they are Black, that does not mean I am going to greet them. I don't greet people I do not know, we are all independent people now. I used to get really upset... I think I was too afraid to understand what was behind it... I think it was too much...

Alicia used to get upset when people greeted her on the street, a strategy she used in order to avoid what she thought might lead to emotional devastation. She didn't feel she would be capable of coping with the connotation of the greeting: Why should Black people greet one another if they do not know each other? Those who were exchanging greetings had never met before, so the greeting was obviously linked not to the present, but to a wound of the collective past, and was a reminder of historical damage that caused Alicia immense anxiety; "We are all independent people now," she says, her strategy for forgetting a past centered around loss and fragmentation.

Personal and collective survival is often based on the repression of the memory of painful past events. In accordance with this, Alicia at first repressed the unacceptable idea of this historicity, arguing that "just because they are Black, that does not mean I am going to greet them." This statement becomes logical only if the idea of the past is forgotten or repressed. Such is the primary function of repression: turning away an unacceptable idea and keeping it at a distance from the conscious because of the anxiety it causes. The idea of having separation and loss at the very center of her experience emerges as a devastating thought. She opposes such an overwhelming possibility: "(...) I am [not] going to greet them. I don't greet people I do not know (...)" The procedure whereby the subject, while formulating a repressed wish or thought, contrives to continue to defend her/himself against it by disowning it, is again *negation* (Laplanche & Pontalis 1988). Alicia can admit the content of the repressed thought – the exchange of greetings – but only in its negative form. The 'no' with which the fact is first denied is immediately followed by a confirmation of it. That is the principle of negation: the repressed idea makes its way into consciousness, but its formulation is negative. Negation therefore marks the bringing to consciousness of repressed material that cannot yet be entirely confessed. According to Freud's interpretation (1923), if we disregard the negation itself and pick out the subject matter independent of the association, we would amend the sentences thus: "I am going to greet them." And finally we could translate them into: "It is true that greeting comes into my mind as I see other Black people, but I don't feel inclined to let the association count." The notion of negation therefore signals the moment when an unconscious idea or wish begins to re-emerge.

28. "(...) SISTAH, HE SAID." – MAMA AFRICA AND TRAUMATIC REPARATION

And once, a young man greeted me on the street and I looked at him very upset and asked: "Excuse me, do we know each other?" And he looked at me and said: "No... sistah!" and kept walking. I was paralyzed... I wanted to get upset, but at the same time it... it touched my heart. He was so natural... and he called me sister, that was so confusing. Sister. It was very... loving. He was a stranger and at that moment I felt how much we had in common, you know... I was a sister and he was my brother, but we didn't know each other – that's too strong. I think that's what I was avoiding all the time... It's like he was saying: "Yes, sistah, I know what you have been through. Me too. But I am here... You are not alone." That's what was in the greeting. It touched me... Nowadays, I usually greet other Black people. It became something natural, I don't even think about it. I have the wish to do that, in a certain way to be in contact with them and in a way to show that we have things common... like our history and being discriminated against...

It was the vocabulary that impressed Alicia. She was called 'sistah.' The term the young man used indicates a common ancestry: the sister shares the same parentage as the brother who addresses her as such. Both are the children of the same mother and/or father and are relatives and members of the same family unit. This terminology, common among African and African Diasporic people, recalls the existence of an imaginary family, a family where all members are brothers and sisters, the children of the same mother continent – Africa.

This idea of an imaginary family leads us back to the concept of trauma and collective fragmentation. The terminology of 'sister' and 'brother' re-creates a sense of unity, illustrating the African continent as a mutilated household and the children of that mutilated household who, as a consequence of having been torn apart, inevitably acknowledge one another as relatives every time they happen to meet. Such acknowledgment is inscribed in both the language and the greeting itself as a clear attempt to work through the colonial trauma of separation. It is a moment of re-unification and a form of piecing together the fragments of a distorted experience.

This re-unification, however, occurs not only on an historical level, but also on an individual one. As Alicia says, "[Nowadays] I have the wish [to greet because] we have things common... like our history and being discriminated against." She speaks of two chronological moments: the past and the present. The greeting and its domestic language heal the wounds of the colonial past, creating a setting in which to overcome the wounds of everyday racism in the present. Indeed African and African Diasporic people have been forced to deal not only with individual trauma, but also with the collective and historical trauma of colonialism, revived and re-actualized by everyday racism. In such an environment, exchanging greetings becomes a short moment – the time for a smile – where one fabricates a setting in which to overcome loss and racial isolation, and at the same time develop a sense of belonging.

CHAPTER 14

DECOLONIZING THE SELF

COLONIAL TRAUMA

To conclude this book, I would like to return to its very beginning: the title, *Plantation Memories*. I want to use the metaphor of the 'plantation' as a symbol of a traumatic past that is restaged through everyday racism. I am therefore speaking of a colonial trauma that has been memorized.

The colonial past is 'memorized' in the sense that it was 'not forgotten.' Sometimes one would prefer not to remember, but one is actually not able to forget. Freud's theory of memory is in reality a theory of forgetting. It assumes that all experiences, or at least all significant experiences, are recorded, but that some cease to be available to the consciousness as a result of repression and to diminish anxiety; others, however, as a result of trauma, remain overwhelming present. One cannot simply forget and one cannot avoid remembering.

The idea of a 'plantation' is furthermore a reminder of a collective history of racial oppression, insult, humiliation and pain, a history that becomes animated in what I call episodes of everyday racism. The thought of 'forgetting' the past becomes indeed unattainable; abruptly, like an alarming shock, one is caught in scenes that evoke the past, but that are actually part of an unreasonable present. This arrangement between past and present is able to depict the unreason of everyday racism as traumatic.

The term trauma is originally derived from the Greek word for 'wound' or 'injury.' The concept of trauma refers to any damage where the skin is broken as a consequence of external violence. Analytically trauma is characterized by a violent event in the subject's life "defined by its intensity, by the subject's inability to respond adequately to it, and by the upheaval and long-lasting effects that it brings about the psychical organisation" (Laplanche & Pontalis 1988: 465). Slavery, colonialism and everyday racism necessarily contain the trauma of an intense and violent life event, an event for which the culture provides no symbolic equivalents and to which the subject is unable to respond adequately because, as Claire Pajaczkowska and Lola Young argue, "the reality of its dehumanization of Black people is one for which there are no adequate words to symbolize it" (1992: 200). Moreover, within the combination of *white* narcissism and negation, the ability to find symbolic equivalents to represent and discharge such a violent reality becomes rather difficult.

Sigmund Freud uses the difficulty of discharging violence as the primary measure for understanding trauma. In *Beyond the Pleasure Principle* (1923), he speaks of a barrier, a protective shield or layer, that allows only tolerable quantities of external excitation through. Should this barrier suffer any breach, trauma results. To label an event traumatic is to assert that a totally unexpected violent experience happened to the subject without her/his willing it in any way or colluding in its occurrence. Slavery, colonialism and everyday racism contain the unexpectedness that leads to injurious effects: injurious because the psychical apparatus cannot "eliminate the excitations in accordance with the principle of constancy" (Laplanche & Pontalis 1988: 467). In economic terms, trauma is characterized by an influx of excitations that exceed the subject's tolerance due to both their violence and unexpectedness; that is, the psychical apparatus is incapable of discharging such excitations because they are disproportionate in relation to the capacity of the psychological organization, whether in the case of a single violent event or an accumulation of violent events. Everyday racism is not a single violent event in one's individual biography, as it is commonly believed – something that "might have happened once or twice" – but rather an accumulation of violent events that at the same time reveal an historical pattern of racial abuse involving not only the horrors of racist violence, but also the collective memories of colonial trauma.

Trauma, however, has rarely been discussed within the context of racism. This absence indicates how Western discourses, and the disciplines of psychology and psychoanalysis in particular, have largely neglected the history of racial oppression and the psychological consequences suffered by the oppressed. Traditional psychoanalysts have failed to acknowledge the influence of social and historical forces on the formation of trauma (Bouson 2000, Fanon 1967). Yet, the painful effects of trauma show that African and African Diasporic people have been forced to deal not only with individual and family trauma within dominant *white* culture, but also with the collective historical trauma of slavery and colonialism restaged in everyday racism, where we again become the subordinate and exotic 'Other' of *white*ness.

TRAUMA AND EVERYDAY RACISM

I would therefore like to conceptualize the experience of everyday racism as traumatic. The psychoanalytical account of trauma carries three main implicit ideas: first, the idea of *a violent shock,* or an unexpected event to which the immediate response is shock; second, *separation* or fragmentation, as this unexpected violent shock deprives one of one's link to society; and third, the idea of *timelessness,* where a violent event that occurred sometime in the past is experienced as if in the present and vice-versa, with painful consequences that affect the whole psychological organization, including nightmares, flashbacks and/or physical pain (Bouson 2000, Kaplan 1999, Laplanche & Pontalis 1988).

In this sense, I will link 'colonial trauma' and 'individual trauma,' and explore the different categories of trauma within everyday racism: (1) violent shock (2) separation and (3) timelessness.

VIOLENT SHOCK

Alicia's experience of having her hair touched by *white* people – "Oh, what interesting hair!" – provides an impressive account of how everyday racism conveys the first element of classic trauma, the violent shock. Alicia remarks upon being unexpectedly addressed as the disposable 'Other' – "I would never touch somebody's hair, just like that" – and is shocked, having not expected to be perceived as such. In that moment of surprise and pain, Alicia tries to find some 'reason' within the 'unreason,' but instead receives more 'unreasonable' answers: "But your hair is different," her mother explains, "and people are just curious!" Alicia cannot apply a 'reasonable' meaning either to the act of being touched or to her mother's answer, as within racism, no agreement "at the level of reason" (Fanon 1967:123) is possible.

In a similar way Kathleen inspiringly narrates her experience of being hailed by a girl, "What a beautiful *N.*!", as a violent shock. "I don't remember the first time that somebody actually physically put their hands on me, to check what Blacks feel like," she says. "But I remember (this) girl talking about '*die schöne Negerin.*'" Kathleen tries to 'rationalize' an 'unreasonable' world that insists on performing the past in the present. But here, there is likewise no agreement possible at the level of reason, as Kathleen is being addressed with the same violent terminology as her ancestors were. She is a '*N.*' "It was up to the white (wo)man to be more irrational than I," writes Fanon (1967: 123).

This sense of shock and unexpectedness is the first element of classic trauma and appears in all episodes of everyday racism. "Oh! No, no!... But you cannot be German," they say, pointing to Alicia's skin. The violent shock resides in not only the fact of being placed as 'Other,' but also in an unreasonable explanation that is difficult to assimilate: "What can you say?" says Alicia. "I actually do not know what I did to overcome this," confesses Kathleen.

There is indeed no agreement at the level of reason; shock is the response to the violent 'unreason' of everyday racism.

This is the first characteristic of classic trauma, any totally unexpected experience that the subject is unable to assimilate and to which the immediate response is shock (Bouson 2000, Laplanche & Pontalis 1988). This is not to say that racism is not expected – unfortunately it is – but the violence and intensity of everyday racism are such that, although expected, they always recreate this element of surprise and shock. In other words, one is never ready to assimilate racism because, as in any other traumatic experience, it is too overwhelming to be "integrated into existing mental frameworks" (van der Kolk 1991: 447). Furthermore, everyday racism is not a single violent event, but rather an accumulation of events that reproduce the trauma of a collective colonial history. The violent shock therefore results from not only the racist assault, but also from the assault of being placed back in a colonial scenario.

After presenting the reader with his traumatic and intense episodes of everyday racism, Fanon tries to work through it by claiming anonymity: "I took myself far off from my own presence, far indeed, and made myself an object" (1967: 112). He continues: "I slip into corners, I remain silent, I strive for anonymity, for invisibility" (1967: 116). To save himself from these expected traumatic assaults, Fanon hopes not to be noticed. He is invited into alienation, as he identifies his own invisibility with equality: a false equation, considering that he can neither escape his Blackness nor the racism surrounding him. And he is aware, confessing that he is surrounded by "(a)ll this whiteness that burns me" (Fanon 1967: 114). Alicia too searches for anonymity in order to escape racist assault: "(S)ometimes I have to ignore (and) pretend I forgot everything," she explains. And at other times "I just do not answer, but then people get very upset... very upset." She might search for anonymity, but she cannot escape the aggression of racism.

The desire to be anonymous also reveals the wish to not be 'haunted' by the trauma of racism. To be traumatized, argues Cathy Caruth, "is precisely to be possessed by an image or an event" (1991: 3). The trauma of having been assaulted by racism becomes a possession, which haunts the subject and repeatedly interrupts one's normal sense of predictability and safety. Kathleen describes this "haunting power" of trauma when she remarkably says, "They are not busy with us, why are we constantly busy with them? Always trying to understand what happened, always thinking, always astonished..." She realizes how she is haunted, possessed by racism. Racism becomes a ghost, haunting us night and day. A ghost in *white*. Because to experience it is too excessive and intolerable to the psychic organization, the violence of racism haunts the Black subject in ways other events do not. It is a strange possession that returns intrusively as fragmented knowledge. One remains haunted by memories and experiences that have caused dehumanizing pain, pain from which one wants to rush away. Everyday racism conveys this first element of trauma, as one is unexpectedly assaulted by a violent event that is experienced as shock and persists in haunting the self.

SEPARATION

"I feel like I have no story at all because my story – the German story, the Afro-German story – is not welcome," says Alicia. "It is as if I have to cut it from myself, to cut my personality, like a schizophrenic. As if some parts of me didn't exist." She describes a sense of separation. The metaphor of having 'to cut herself' or 'cut her personality' conveys the second element of classic trauma; it indicates the sense of break, cutting and loss caused by the violence of everyday racism, an unexpected shock that deprives one of one's link with society. "Where are you from? Why do you speak German that good?" Such questions break Alicia's link to a society unconsciously thought of as *white*. Her sense of belonging is damaged, as she is violently assaulted and separated from society. "Look how nice the *N.* looks." Kathleen describes the sense of separation resulting from the violent shock of being placed as 'Other.' Her reality is fragmented, as she is separated from others by racism. The *white* girl, the *white* mother and the *white* boyfriend are one, while Kathleen is the 'Other.' In classic trauma, links to other humans, to a sense of community or to a group, so basic to human identity, are lost (Bouson 2000). Twice Kathleen is separated from the community: first, because she becomes a '*N.*' while those surrounding her do not, and second, because, in becoming one of the '*N.*'s, she is in another sub-category of humanity. She is separated twice, inside the room and again outside the room. "On that day, completely dislocated," writes Fanon, "unable to be abroad with the Other, the white man, who unmercifully imprisoned me, I took myself far off from my presence, far indeed, and made myself an object" (Fanon 1967: 112). Fanon's sense of community and his link to others are radically disrupted. This sense of fragmentation coincides with the historical fragmentation of slavery and colonialism, a history centered on the drama of disunion, separation and isolation. It is no accident that in her last publications – *All About Love: New Visions* (2000) and *Salvation: Black People and Love* (2001) –

bell hooks writes about love and union as a political project for Black people. hooks argues that the autobiographies of enslaved Africans "tell a collective story of individuals emotionally ravaged by separation from homeland, clan, and family." When emotional ties were established between individuals, or "when children were born to enslaved mothers and fathers, these attachments were often severed. No matter the tenderness of connection, it was often overshadowed by the trauma of abandonment and loss" (2001: 19-20). The narratives of enslaved and colonized people document the efforts Black people made to normalize life in a fragmented reality. Because of this historical fragmentation and its overwhelming sense of separation, love and union emerge as a political assignment to repair our individual and collective historicity of loss and isolation. As one has been and is still deprived of one's link to society, causing an internal sense of loss, this idea of unity is used as a political movement to overcome separation, the second element of trauma.

TIMELESSNESS: PAST AND PRESENT

All of the episodes reveal a sense of timelessness, as one is being addressed in the present as if one were in the past. "How do you wash your hair? Do you comb it?" Alicia is being perceived through an old colonial gaze: "Negros are savages, brutes, illiterates" (Fanon 1967: 117). In shock, Alicia tries first to respond to this assault with certain amusement: "What a question. How do I wash my hair? Well, with water and shampoo, like everyone else," she says, laughing. But this laughter becomes impossible to sustain. "I ask myself, what is it that they really want to say (...) I don't know... Well, I know, but I do not even want to think about it." She cannot laugh anymore, as racism is not a matter of laughter, but of pain. There is indeed nothing to laugh about. "Look at you, look at your hair, you look like a sheep!" "Why don't you do your hair?" "Do you know what a comb is?!" The violence escalates as the present approaches the past. It is as if Alicia is transported somewhere else in history, being addressed as if it were a century ago. She is not here anymore. Or at least 'here' feels like 'back then.'

This sense of immediacy and presence is the third element of classic trauma. An event that occurred sometime in the past is experienced as if it were happening in the present and vice-versa: the event occurring in the present is experienced as if one were in the past. Colonialism and racism come to coincide. "I remember feeling for the first time... this kind of physical pain as I heard that word," says Kathleen. The past assaults her in the present. As soon as she heard the *N*-word, she says, "I got this ache in my fingers." Kathleen is haunted by the traumatic past, which "returns intrusively as fragmented sensory or motoric experiences" (van der Kolk and van der Hart 1991: 447). One is haunted by intrusive colonial memories, which tend to return.

Slavery and colonialism may be seen as things of the past, but they are intimately bound to the present. In *Ghosts of Slavery*, Jenny Sharpe (2003) emphasizes the link between the past and the present, a present haunted by the intrusive past of slavery. She refers to slavery as a 'haunting of history' that continues to disturb the present lives of Black people. Her purpose, she says, is to resuscitate the lives of the ancestors by raising the painful memory of slavery and telling it properly. This is an alluring association: our history haunts us because it has been improperly buried. Writing is, in this sense, a way to resuscitate a traumatic collective experience and bury it properly. The idea of an improper burial is identical to the idea of a traumatic event that could not be discharged properly and therefore still exists vividly and intrusively in our present minds. Hence timelessness, on the one hand, describes the past co-existing with the present, and on the other hand describes how the present co-exists with the past. Everyday racism places us back in scenes of a colonial past – colonizing us again.

DECOLONIZATION

Decolonization refers to the undoing of colonialism. Politically, the term describes the achievement of autonomy by those who have been colonized and therefore involves the realization of both independence and self-determination.

The idea of decolonization can be easily applied in the context of racism because everyday racism establishes a dynamic similar to colonialism itself: one is looked at, spoken to, assaulted, injured and finally imprisoned in *white* fantasies of what one should be like. To translate these five moments into militaristic colonial language, one is discovered, invaded, attacked, subjugated and occupied. Being 'looked at' becomes analogous to being 'discovered'; etc.

In a matter of seconds, a colonial maneuver is performed upon the Black subject, who symbolically becomes colonized. I indeed like this metaphor of everyday racism as an act of colonization because colonialism lies exactly in the extension of a nation's sovereignty over a territory beyond its borders

– and this is also how everyday racism is experienced. One feels as if one is being appropriated by the *white* others who, without permission, "walk in your direction and ask [where you come from] without even knowing you," according to Alicia, or "touch our hair or our skin to see what Blacks feels like," according to Kathleen. It does not matter where you are: "in a bus, at a party, on the street, a dinner or even at the supermarket." Alicia and Kathleen describe everyday racism as a *white* ritual of colonial conquest, as they feel they are being invaded like a piece of land. Their bodies are explored like continents, their stories given new names, their languages changed; and above all, they see themselves being shaped by intrusive fantasies of subordination. For a moment they become metaphorical colonies.

It seems the *white* subject has an urge to recover its object of loss. In a state of grief and despair, the *white* subject performs a ritual of colonial occupation, rejecting the idea that such loss has occurred. It protests against it: "I say that I am German," says Alicia. "Oh! No, no! But you cannot be German," they answer desperately trying to restore the loss of a colonial past. While the *white* subject restages the past, the Black subject is forbidden the present. This is the function of everyday racism, to restage a colonial order that has been lost, but can be revived the moment the Black subject is placed again as the 'Other.'

Because the *white* subject does not want to get over the loss of the past – that is, the loss of both colonialism and the idea of *white* supremacy – it is also not capable of re-attaching itself to the idea of racial equality. The present and the idea of equality are refused and instead prevail the fantasy that the past will triumph. We are dealing here with a state of colonial mourning, as the *white* subject feels incredulous and angry that racial 'Others' might become equals to *whites*. One is indeed caught in an act of colonialism that one necessarily has to 'undo.'

This is the moment in which both colonization and decolonization become intertwined and imperative. But how does this process of 'undoing' take place? How does one decolonize her/himself? What should the decolonization of the self look like? And which questions should be asked in order to find possible answers? Should I ask, for instance, what you did after the incident of racism? Or should I instead ask what the incident of racism did with you? Should the focus be the reply or rather the reflection? The performance toward the *white* other or the feelings toward oneself?

"WHAT DID YOU DO?" vs. "WHAT DID RACISM DO WITH YOU?"

One does not have to choose one or the other. But remembering that everyday racism has been massively negated in our society and that those who experience it are constantly reminded to not name it, to keep it quiet, as a secret – in this sense, the question "what did the incident do with you" is quite liberating. It makes room for what has been denied.

It is common to insist upon what one did –"What did you do afterward?" – but not upon what racism did to oneself. The myth that Black people victimize themselves when they speak about the wounds caused by racism is a very effective strategy to silence those who are ready to speak. The question "what did racism do with you" has nothing to do with victimization; it has to do with empowerment, as one becomes the speaking subject, speaking of one's own reality. I have been concerned not with the question "what did you do," but rather with "what did racism do with you." I indeed see this question as a real act of decolonization and political resistance in that it allows the Black subject to finally be busy with her/himself instead of with the *white* other. The question is directed to the inside (what – did *it* do – with *you)* and not to the outside (what – did *you* do – with *them*). That is for me quite revolutionary.

As mentioned above, everyday racism imprisons the Black subject in a colonial order that forced one to exist only through the alienating presence of the *white* subject. The question "what did you do" tends to force the Black subject to develop a relationship to her/himself through that other, by asking about one's own performance toward the *white* audience. One is invited to be busy again with what the *white* subject should hear, how to conquer her/him and how to be understood by her/him – creating a virtual dependency.

This does not mean that the question itself is irrelevant, but it should be secondary rather than primary, as it might imprison us in that colonial order again.

DEPENDENCY vs. INDEPENDENCY: SETTING NEW BORDERS

Alicia describes this dependency quite well when she argues trying to explain to her *white* audience that she is indeed German, but, pointing to her skin, they insist upon her foreignness. She tries to explain again and again, but they keep asking. Alicia has to realize that she is caught in an act of colonization; the conflict resides not in the answer she gives, but rather in the joyful power of invading her – and making her dependent. Kathleen describes this *white* dependency when at work her colleagues keep asking her where she comes from: "I am from the US," she replies. "Yes, but your parents?" "They are from the US." "And your grandparents, where are they from? And your great-grandparents?" Kathleen is questioned over and over again. The questionnaire, which Kathleen experiences as invasive, reveals how it is not her answers that are actually important, but the act of invasion itself. Those who ask are interested not in her responses, but rather in the experience of occupying the Black subject with themselves. Here, whiteness emerges as a dependent identity, compulsively wanting to invade, occupy and possess the Black subject as its 'Other.'

If on the one hand the *white* subject seems to be obsessed with the idea of invading the Black subject, the Black subject, on the other hand, has to come to the conclusion that racism is not a lack of information, but rather a violent desire to possess and control the Black subject. It is an invasive act with elements of dependency: the *white* subject asks and the Black subject answers, the *white* subject requests and the Black subject explains, the *white* subject demands and the Black subject elucidates. We can explain but within racism the aim is not to understand, but to possess and control. In other words, the aim is not to find the answer, but rather the amusing act of keeping the Black subject dependent on the *white* self.

Alicia later confesses how she used to explain herself continuously and tell her story in detail, but had to realize that actually "(t)hey don't want to hear it or know about it [...] Sometimes I do not answer at all." By not answering Alicia removes herself from that colonial scene and in doing so, sets new boundaries in her relationship to the *white* other: *I do not answer because my answer would be my imprisonment in your colonial order.* Alicia is both setting new limits (*Grenzen setzen*) and delimiting herself from others (*sich abgrenzen*). Similarly Kathleen warns her neighbhor about the doll she exhibits on her balcony. "I explained to her that there are three women of color living next door and we thought it was a piece of shit," says Kathleen. "And all of our Black friends who are coming to visit us have to look at it too, and it was offensive to us, and it was invading our space, she is playing with something very serious. (So) if she's going to keep it on her balcony, she also needs to make sure that she knows that." Kathleen is both setting the limits and delimiting herself from the neighbor. She is not really explaining herself, but rather defining the new boundaries of the relationship between herself and the *white* woman, defining her place in this Black and *white* relationship: "Two weeks later she put a little plastic cover around it." Kathleen succeeded because she left the colonial constellation.

To explain is to nourish a colonial order, as one speaks and the *white* subject may always say that disdainful sentence: "Yes, but..." And one explains again, and again one hears the sentence: "Yes, but..." And this invasive and dependent cycle never ends. As everyday racism is invasive, it seems that it is the setting of boundaries that leads to one's own decolonization, not the explanation. While incessantly explaining her/himself, the Black subject expands her/his borders instead of setting new borders. To achieve a new role as equal, one also has to place her/himself outside the colonial dynamic; that is, one has to say farewell to that place of Otherness. It is therefore an important task for the Black subject to say farewell (*sich zu verabschieden*) to the fantasy of having to explain her/himself to the *white world*.

WANTING TO BE UNDERSTOOD vs. UNDERSTANDING: CHANGING THE TRIANGLE

One explains because one wants to be understood. But to whom is one explaining? And by whom does one want to be understood? By the aggressor? By the *white* audience, who has observed the incident of racism? Or maybe both? And why is it important to be understood by the *white* other? This arrangement implies a triangle. Everyday racism is performed in a triangular constellation in which the Black subject is singled out. There are always three elements included in this performance: the *white* subject who insults, the Black subject who is insulted, and the *white* audience who usually observes silently, representing the *white* consensus. Here, I am concerned with the fantasy of wanting to be understood by the *white* consensus.

Kathleen describes this fantasy when she sees the Black doll on her neighbor's balcony for the first time. Her first concern is to be understood: "I and my roommate were trying to decide what we should do about it, if we should throw things at it or write anonymous letters." It seems Kathleen is unsure about what to do, not because she doubts that it is racist, but because unconsciously she desires to be understood by the *white* woman. There is disharmony between what racism does with her and what she does with it. Kathleen knows what racism has caused her – fury – but at first she is unclear about what response to eventually give. She hesitates to use her anger and fury as resources to negotiate everyday racism; instead, she gets confused. We often confuse feelings; sometimes we feel a fervent anger and annoyance, but express sadness and helplessness instead. Or we carry a deep wound, but express constant anger and irritation instead. We confuse feelings, not because we don't understand, but rather because we desire to be understood.

What would happen if we allowed ourselves to feel the rage caused by racism? What would we have to do with that anger? Or with that desolation? And what would the *white* subject have to listen to? We strongly invest in the fantasy that we should be understood in order to avoid a sense of disillusionment and conflict. Often, however, we are not understood, especially when we speak out against racism. We have to sadly realize that we cannot always change the *white* consensus, but instead we have to change our relation toward it. This demands understanding instead of wanting to be understood. "(A)nd I thought: 'Today is the day!'" says Kathleen. She decides not to change the *white* woman but rather her relationship toward the woman – as her fury is more evident than her wish to be understood by the neighbor. The *white* woman also wants to be understood, as she claims to have a Cuban friend who likes the doll, just as she does. Kathleen, however, has no more understanding for racism. Instead she uses her anger as resource, as anger helps one to know what one wants and does not want: "(I want to tell you that this doll is) offensive."

Likewise, Alicia says, "(W)hen I was twenty-one I told my parents not to use the *N*-word, until then I was never able to talk about it... they would say (...) I am too sensitive." Alicia describes how she ends the fantasy of wanting to be understood by her parents. The end of this second fantasy coincides with the moment that, instead of wanting to change the *white* consensus, Alicia changes her role toward it. Kathleen and Alicia both change the initial triangulation. "I read a lot, to learn, to study... I read many books... meet other Black people and realized they had experienced the same," says Alicia. "So when I was able to define myself as Black and stopped calling myself all those awful names. Yes..!"

PERFECTIONISM VS. AUTONOMY: DISALIENATION

Another fantasy is that if one makes enough of an effort to explain, one will be accepted and will thus escape the violence of everyday racism. I am therefore talking about the fantasy of perfectionism toward the *white* audience and how this again imprisons the Black subject in a colonial order: "I should have said that instead... No, next time, you should say this... What do you say when they ask you where you are from? What do you do when..?

151

No, no, no, next time you say..." One is caught in a state of permanent servitude, as one seeks to deliver the perfect answer to the *white* subject.

On the one hand, this fantasy of perfection allows the Black subject to repair what has been destroyed, as one re-establishes stolen authority by becoming justly authoritative: *Now I have such a good answer, you are going be amazed. I will knock you out!* The fantasy of being perfect responds to the anxiety that a racist disaster might occur again at any minute. This time, however, one is prepared – one will not be destroyed by racism. Fantasizing about having an excellent response calms the fear of being attacked again by *white* sadism. Due to its cleverness and coolness, the good answer is thought of as a weapon to disarm the *white* other. This can indeed be regarded as an act of reparation since the Black subject recreates her/his self as powerful; and in this sense, it can be seen as a creative activity by which one resolves an incident of everyday racism.

This fantasy of perfection, however, is not really gratifying. It leads to a constant state of disappointment. One has to realize that everyday racism is an unexpected violent assault and that one is suddenly caught by the shock of its violence, and in this sense, one cannot always answer. The idea of a 'perfect' response cultivates the idea of an *ideal* ego, an ego that reacts accordingly every time the *white* subject acts. A very ungratifying fantasy, as no one can achieve such a state of idealism and perfection.

Moreover, this fantasy cultivates the idea of servitude. While the *white* other acts, the Black subject is reduced to reacting to *white*ness. While *white*ness can be incoherent and faulty, Blackness is expected to be perfect and precise. Investing in the fantasy that one should deliver the 'right answer' may come to resemble maniac defenses and sometimes obsessive ones. In this fantasy, one is comparable to an heroic character who has 'the answer' to several unpredictable attacks. This is, of course, an absolute contradiction of the fact that racism is a traumatic experience to which sometimes the only possible response is shock. And above all, a contradiction of the fact that we are also humans: "I do not want to be super-human any more than I want to be sub-human," says Kathleen. "(W)hen I am angry, I want to have the freedom of being angry, and when I am weak, I would like to have the freedom of being weak." Kathleen associates this idea of perfectionism with the concept of alienation, as one has to exist as an alienating image of oneself, whether created by *white*s or created in opposition to *white*ness. Kathleen instead wants to exist in all her complexity: as angry, as quiet; as strong, as weak; as joyful, as sad; as knowing the answers, as not knowing at all.

This complexity reveals the fact that in reality, one does not always have 'the answer' – and that is the answer itself. There are several answers, on several days, according to several moods, and depending on several circumstances. And we should feel free to allow this complexity to exist. 'The answer' does not exist as such, but rather several answers – and among these, no answer at all. Bidding farewell to this fantasy of perfection is the third crucial task for the Black subject, in order to arrive at neither the dis-idealized 'Other' nor the idealized 'Other,' but at the complex self.

BECOMING A SUBJECT

I would like to conclude with a sequence of ego defense mechanisms the Black subject goes through in order to become aware of her/his Blackness and experienced reality with everyday racism, as they became obvious in the biographies of both Alicia and Kathleen. I use ego defense mechanisms, for the function of the defense is to protect the ego from the conflicts with the outside. It is a general designation for all the techniques the ego uses to master outside reality. There are therefore five different ego defense mechanisms: negation / frustration / ambivalence / identification / decolonization.

Negation, as mentioned earlier, is the ego defense mechanism in which an experience is only admitted to the conscious in its negative form. For instance, although the Black subject experiences racism, the information contained in such statements as "I do experience racism," "I am Black" or "I am treated different" causes so much anxiety that they are formulated in the negative: "I <u>never</u> experience racism," "I am <u>not</u> really Black" or "I am <u>not</u> treated different." Negation thus protects the subject from the anxiety certain information causes once it is admitted to the conscious. As we are taught to speak with the language of the oppressor, in negation the Black subject speaks with the words of the *white* other: "There is <u>no</u> racism," "I <u>don't</u> want to define myself as Black, because we are all humans" or "I think in our society there is <u>no</u> differences."

Frustration is the state of being, or having been, balked, baffled or disappointed; Malcolm X speaks of being 'bamboozled.' The Black subject comes to realize her/his deprivation in the *white* conceptual world. Such deprivation leads to effects of dissatisfaction or failure to achieve one's own personal goals: so-called frustration. "Even though I want to believe that 'race' does not matter, I have to admit that I do experience racism," "Even though I am told that we are all equal, I have to admit that I am treated different."

Frustration refers therefore to the lack of opportunities necessary for satisfaction, the Black subject is unsatisfied for she/he realizes that she/he does not have the same opportunities as the *white* consensus. One is frustrated with both the *white* other and *white* society in general. The sequence of frustration is – aggression – anxiety – defense and – inhibition.

Ambivalence usually refers to the co-existence of love and hate. After experiencing frustration, one is left with ambivalent feelings toward the *white* subject. Ambivalence does not mean one has mixed feelings about an object; it refers instead to an underlying emotional attitude in which the contradictory opinions derive from the same source. One feels anger and guilt toward *whites*, disgust and hope, trust and distrust. Pride and guilt toward Blacks, solidarity and shame, confidence and doubt: two contradictory feelings in relation to a single object. This stage is a preparation to identification: with whom should I identify myself?

Identification refers to the process in which the subject "assimilates an aspect of the other and is transformed, wholly or partly, after the model the other provides" (Laplanche and Pontalis 1988: 205). In this state the Black subject starts a series of consecutive identifications with other Black people: their history, their biographies, their experiences, their knowledge, etc. These series of identifications prevent the Black subject from the alienating identification with whiteness. Instead of identifying with the *white* other, one develops a positive identification with one's own Blackness, leading to a sense of inner security and self-recognition. Such process leads to reparation and openness toward *whites*, since internally one is outside the colonial order. The whole process achieves a state of *decolonization*; that is, internally one exists no longer as the 'Other,' but as the self. One is the self, one is the subject, one is the describer, the author of and the authority on one's own reality. As I started this book: one becomes the subject.

"Kuá cu tê tocá nguê suba ná cá sobê lá béfá."
"What is ours will not be taken by the rain."
(a traditional proverb from São Tomé and Príncipe)

LITERATURE

Ahmed, Sara (2000), *Strange Encounters. Embodied Others in Post-Coloniality*. London: Routeledge.

Anthias, Floya & Yuval-Davis, Nira (1992), *Racialized boundaries. Race, nation, gender, colour and class and the anti-racist struggle*. New York: Routledge.

Arndt, Susan & Hornscheidt, Antje (Hg.) (2004), *Afrika und die deustche Sprache*. Münster: Unrast Verlag

Ayim, May (1997), *Grenzlos und unverschämt*. Berlin: Orlanda Verlag.

Banks, Ingrid (2000), *Hair Matters. Beauty, Power, and Black Women's Consciousness*. New York: New York Univesity Press.

Barker, Martin (1981), *The New Racism*. London: Junction Books.

Bhabha, Homi (1986), "Remembering Fanon," foreword to Frantz Fanon: *Black Skin, White Masks*. London: Grove Press.

Bouson, J. Brooks (2000), *Quiet as it's Kept. Shame, Trauma, and Race in the Novels of Toni Morrison*.New York: SUNY Press.

Byrd, Ayana D. & Tharps, Lori L. (2001), *Hair Story. Untangling the Roots of Black Hair in America*.New York: St. Martins Press.

Carby, Hazel V. (1997), White Women listen! In Heidi Safia Mirza (ed.) *Black British Feminism. A Reader*. London: Routledge.

Caruth, Cathy (1991), "Introduction." *Psychoanalysis, Culture and Trauma*. Ed. Cathy Caruth. Spec. Issues of *American Imago* 48.1 (Spring 1991): 1-12.

Castro Varela, Maria del Mar & Dhawan, Nikita (2003), Postkolonialer Feminismus und die Kunst der Selbstkritik. In Hito Steyerl & Encarnación Gutiérrez Rodríguez (Hg.) *Spricht die Subalterne deutsch? Migration und postkoloniale kritik*. (pp. 270-290). Münster: UNRAST Verlag.

Collins, Patricia Hill (2000), *Black Feminist Thought. Knowledge, Consciousness, and the Politics of Empowerment*. New York: Routledge.Derrida, Jacques (1981), *Positions*. Chicago: University of Chicago Press.

Derrida, Jacques (1981), *Positions*. Chicago: University of Chicago Press.

Essed, Philomena (1990), *Everyday Racism. Reports from Women of Two Cultures*. Hunter House Publishers.

Essed, Philomena (1991), *Understanding Everyday Racism. An Interdisciplinary Theory*. London: Routledge.

Fanon, Frantz (1967), *Black Skin, White Masks*. London: Grove Press.

Feagin, Joe R. & Jean, ST. Yannick (1998), *Double Burden. Black Women and Everyday Racism*. New York: M.E. Sharpe.

Freud, Sigmund (1923), *The Ego and the Id and Other Works (1923-1925) Vol. XIX*. London: Vintage.

Fulani, Lenora (1988), *The Psychopathology of Everyday Racism and Sexism*. NewYork: Harrington Park Press.

Gaber, Ivor & Aldridge, Jane (eds.) (1994), *In the Best interest of the Child. Culture, Identity and Transracial Adoption*. London: Free Association Books.

Gaines, Jane (2001), White privilege and looking relations: race and gender in feminist film theory. In Jessica Evans and Stuart Hall (eds.) *Visual Culture: the reader.* London: SAGE.

Gilroy, Paul (1987), *'There Ain't No Black in the Union Jack':* The cultural Politics of race and nation. London: Hutchinson.

Gilroy, Paul (1992), "The end of anti-racism" in James Donald & Ali Rattansi (Eds). *"Race," Culture and Difference* (pp. 49-61). London: SAGE

Hall, Stuart (1990), Cultural Identity and Diaspora. In Jonathan Rutherford (ed). *Identity, Community, Culture, Difference.* London: Lawrence & Wishart Limited, pp. 222-237.

Hall, Stuart (1992), New Ethnicities. In James Donald & Ali Rattansi (eds). *'Race', Culture and Difference.* London: SAGE, pp. 252-259.

Hall, Stuart, (1996), The After-life of Franzt Fanon: Why Fanon? Why Now? Why Black Skin, White Masks? In Alan Read (eds.) *The Fact of Blackness. Frantz Fanon and Visual Representation.* (pp. 12-37). London: Bay Press.

Handler, Jerome & Hayes, Kelly (2009), Escrava Anastácia: The Iconographic History of a Braziian Popular Saint. *African Diaspora* 2: 25-51.

hooks, bell (1981), *Ain't I a Woman. Black Women and Feminism.* Boston: South End Press.

hooks, bell (1989), *Talking Back: Thinking Feminist, Talking Black.* Boston: South End Press.

hooks, bell (1990), *Yearning. Race, Gender and Cultural Politics.* Boston: South End Press.

hooks, bell (1992), *Black Looks. Race and Representation.* London: Turnaround.

hooks, bell (1994), *Teaching to Transgress. Education as the Practice of Freedom.* London: Routledge.

hooks, bell (1995), *Killing Rage. Ending Racism.* New York: Owl Books.

hooks, bell (2000), *All About Love. New Visions.* New York: HarperCollins books.

hooks, bell (2001), *Salvation. Black people and Love.* London: Cox & Wyman.

Hügel-Marshal, Ika (2001), *Daheim unterwegs. Eine deutsches Leben.*Frankfurt am Main: Fischer Tachenbuch Verlag.

Jelloun, Tahar Ben (1998). *Le Racisme Expliqué à ma Fille.* Paris: Editions du Seuil.

Kaplan, E. Ann (1999), Fanon, Trauma and Cinema. In Anthony C. Alessandrini (ed.) *Frantz Fanon. Critical Perspectives.* London: Routledge.

Kennedy, Randall (2002), *Nigger. The Strange Carrer of a Troublesome Word.* New York: First Vintage Books.

Kilomba, Grada (2003), Die Kolonizierung des Selbst – der Platz des Schwarzen. In Hito Steyerl & Encarnacíon Gutiérrez Rodriguez (Hg.) *Spricht die Subaltern deutsch? Migration und postkoloniale kritik.* Münster: Unrast Verlag.

Kilomba, Grada (2004), "Don't You Call Me '*Neger*'!" – Das N-Wort, Trauma und Rassismus. In AntiDiskriminierungsBüro (ADB) Köln von Öffentlichkeit gegen Gewalt e.V. & cybernomads (cbN), *TheBlackBook. Deutschlands Häutungen.*Frankfurt-Lodon: IKO Verlag.

Kilomba, Grada (2005), No Mask. In Maureen Maisha Eggers, Grada Kilomba, Peggy Piesche & Susan Arndt, *Masken, Mythen und Subjekte. Weißseinforchung in Deutschland*. Münster: Unrast Verlag.

Laplanche, Jean & Pontalis, Jean-Bertrand (1988), *The Language of Psychoanalysis*. London: Polestar Wheatons Ltd.

Loomba, Ania (1998), *Colonialism/Postcolonialism*. London: Routledge.

Lorde, Audre (1993), *Black Unicorn*. New York: Norton & Co.

Mama, Amina (1995), *Beyond the Masks. Race, Gender and Subjectivity*. London: Routledge.

Marriot, David (1998), Bonding Over Phobia. In Christopher Lane. *The Psychoanalysis of Race*. New York: Columbia.

Mecheril, Paul (1997), Halb-halb. *iza, Zeitschrift für Migration und Sozial Arbeit*. thema 3-4.

Mecheril, Paul (1998), Rassismuserfahrungen. In Siegfried Grubitzsch & Klaus Weber (Hg.) *Psychologische Grundbegriffe. Ein Handbuch*. Hamburg: rowohlts enzyklopädie.

Mecheril, Paul (2000), "Ist doch egal, was man macht, man ist aber trotzdem 'n Ausländer" – Formen von Rassismuserfahrungen. In W.D. Butow (Hrsg) Familie im .... globaler Migration.

Mercer, Kobena (1994), *Welcome to the Jungle. New Positions in Black Cultural Studies*. London: Routledge.

Mirza, Heidi Safia (ed.)(1997), *Black British Feminism. A Reader*. London: Routledge.

Mohanram, Radhika (1999), *Black Body. Women, Colonialism and Space*. Minneapolis: University of Minnesota Press.

Morrison, Toni (1992), *Playing in the Dark. Whiteness and the Literary Imagination*. New York: Vintage Books.

Nkweto Simmonds, Felly (1997), My Body, myself: How does a Black woman do sociology? In Heidi Safia Mirza (ed.) *Black British Feminism. A Reader*.London: Routledge.

Oguntoye, Katharina; Opitz, May & Schultz, Dagmar (eds.)(1986), *Farbe bekennen. Afrodeutsche Frauen auf den Spuren ihrer Geschichte*. Frankfurt: Fischer.

Oguntoye, Katharina (1997), *Eine afro-deutsche Geshchte. Zur Lebensituation von Afrikanern und Afro-Deutschen in Deutschland von 1884 bis 1950*.Berlin: Hoho Verlag.

Pajaczkowska, Claire & Young, Lola (1992), Racism, Representation, Psychoanalysis. In James Donald & Ali Rattansi. *'Race', Culture and Difference*. London: SAGE.

Rattansi, Ali (1994), 'Western' Racisms, Ethnicities and Identities in a 'Postmodern' Frame. In Ali Rattansi & Sallie Westwood (Eds). *Racism, Modernity and Identity in the Western Front* (pp.15-86). London: SAGE.

Reed-Andersoon, Paulette (2000), *Rewritng the Footnotes. Berlin and the African Diaspora*. Berlin: Commisionaire for Foreigners' Affairs.

Reynolds, Tracey (1997), (Mis)representating the black (super)woman. In Heidi Safia Mirza (ed.) *Black British Feminism. A Reader*. London: Routledge.

Sam-La Rose, Jacob, (2002) In *Sable*. Winter, p.60.

Sernhede, Ove (2000), Gangsta Rap and the Search for Intensity. In Paul Gilroy, Lawrence Grossberg & Angela McRobbie (Eds.) *Without Guarantees. In Honour of Start Hall*. London:Verso

Sharpe, Jenny (2003), *Ghosts of Slavery. A Literary Archeology of Black Women's Lives*. London: University of Minnesota Press.

Smith, Barbara (ed.) (1983), *Home Girls*. New York: Kitchen Table Press.

Spivak, Gayatri Chakravarty (1993), *Outside in the Teaching Machine*. London: Routledge.

Spivak, Gayatri Chakravarty (1995), Can the Subaltern Speak? In Bill Ashcroft, Gareth Griffiths & Helen Tiffin (Eds.), *The post-colonial studies reader* (pp.24-28). London: Routledge.

Staeuble, Irmingard (2007), Entangled in the Eurocentric Order of Knowledge – Why psychology is difficult to decolonise. In Vasi van Deventer, Martin Terre Blanche, Eduard Fourie and Puleng Segalo, *Citizen City. Between constructing agent and deconstructed agency*. Captus University Publications.

Steyerl, Hito & Rodriguez, Encarnación Gutiérrez (ed.) (2003), *Spricht die Subalterne deutsch? Migration und postkoloniale kritik.*Münster: Unrast Verlag.

Tizard, Barbara & Phoenix, Ann (1993), *Black, white or mixed 'race'? 'Race' and racism in the lives of people of mixed parentage*. London: Routledge.

Weiß, Anja (1998), Rassismus. In Siegfried Grubitzsch & Klaus Weber (Hg.) *Psychologische Grundbegriffe. Ein Handbuch*. Hamburg: rowohlts enzyklopädie.

West, Cornel (1995), The New Cultural Politics of Difference. In John Rajchman (ed.) *The Identity in Question*. London: Routledge.

Young, Lola (1996), Mission Persons: Fantasising Black Women in Black Skin, White Masks. In Alan Read (Ed.), *The Fact of Blackness. Frantz Fanon Visual Representation.* (pp. 86-101). London: Bay Press.

van der Kolk, Bessel & van der Hart, Onno (1991), "The Intrusive Past: The Flexibility of Memory and the Engraving of Trauma." *American Imago*, 48.4 (Winter 1991): 425-54.

INDEX